RADICAL RELATIONSHIP RESOURCE

RADICAL RELATIONSHIP RESOURCE

A GUIDE FOR REPAIRING, LETTING GO, OR MOVING ON

Carol Morgan, Ph.D.
Dick Sutphen

Companion E-Courses to this Book

Relationship Complaints & Solutions E-Courses:
Parts One, Two, & Three

Other E-Courses Available:
Create Your Life: A Law of Attraction E-Course Series
The Critical 15—A Relationship Renewal System:
Parts One, Two, Three, Four, & Five
All E-Courses are available at *DrCarolMorgan.com*

Other Books

We're Not That Different:
Two Sisters' Religious & Spiritual Journeys
by Carol Morgan, Ph.D.
You Were Born Again to Be Together by Dick Sutphen
Past Lives, Future Loves by Dick Sutphen
Predestined Love by Dick Sutphen
Finding Your Answers Within by Dick Sutphen

Find more services
by Dr. Carol Morgan & Dick Sutphen at:
DrCarolMorgan.com & RichardSutphen.com

Infinity One Publishing

First Edition

ISBN:9780615901466

Cover and text design by Alicia Fox (www.aliciafoxdesign.com)

Dedication

To Colton & Chase.
May you find true happiness in your relationships…*always.*
I love you both more than anything in the whole world.

To the Sutphen clan—you all have my heart.

Table of Contents

How To Use This Book ix

SECTION ONE Common Complaints of Relationship Demise 1

SECTION TWO 'Maintenance & Repair' Tips 29

For people who are:

- Currently in a relationship
- Who want a relationship, and will probably be in one in the near future.

SECTION THREE 'Letting Go & Moving On' Tips 127

For people who are:

- Thinking about getting out of a relationship
- Have broken up and need to move on in a healthy manner
- Want to create a better relationship the next time

How To Use This Book

After many collective years of research, writing, teaching, and conducting seminars, we know first-hand that people need significant help in the area of relationships. Naturally, because our careers deal with the public, we hear all about their problems. Although they are all slightly different, there are definitely core similarities.

Some people are trying to maintain or repair their current union, while others are attempting to let go and move on. Frequently, they turn to relationship/self-help books. Most of these deal with psychological or communication issues within relationships. But we wanted to write a book that is slightly different in form and content. In order to do this, we decided to incorporate some controversial topics. They might be considered "radical" by most people because they are not generally accepted by our society. For example, some of the repairs deal with applying metaphysical spirituality to your relationship, and others deal with sexual alternatives to monogamy. Hopefully, some of what we've written will push you out of your comfort zone and start considering some new ideas. Because without new ideas, there can be no growth.

We also wanted to make the format different. Everyone has a busy life, and it is hard to find the time to sit down and read a book from cover to cover. Therefore, we decided to get radical with how we formatted the book. Perhaps not radical, but certainly different than what most readers are used to reading.

Although we organized the book into different phases of relationship status, we assure you that everyone will benefit from the ideas in this book. For example, if you are not currently in a relationship, you will still be able to use the "Maintenance & Repairs" tips in the future.

We hope you enjoy our book. Our joint intention is to serve humanity, and if this book changes even one person's life for the better, it will all be worth it.

SECTION ONE

COMMON COMPLAINTS OF RELATIONSHIP DEMISE

Table of Contents

SECTION ONE COMMON COMPLAINTS OF RELATIONSHIP DEMISE

Adultery/Cheating 4
Third Party Distraction 5
Sexual Incompatibility 6
Financial Disagreement/Hardship 7
In-Law Interference 8
Blended Families 9
Not Enough Time Together 10
Immaturity/Selfishness/
Lack of Ambition 11
Failed Expectations Or Unmet Needs 12
No Fun or Romance 13
Poor Communication 14
Control Issues 15
Shared Responsibility Issues 16
Addictions Or Substance Abuse 17
Incompatible Friends 18
Lack of Emotional Support 19
Constant Arguing 20
Lack Of Commitment 21
Incompatible Goals/Values 22
Lack of Trust, Jealousy
Or Possessiveness 23
Lifestyle Differences 24
Abusive Behavior 25
No Longer In-Love with Mate 26
Your Mate "Changed" 27
No Appreciation 28

What is the difference between the 'Radical' & 'General' Viewpoints?

In this first section of the book, we discuss 25 of the most common relationship complaints that lead to demise.

1. We describe the **COMMON CAUSES** of each of these complaints.
2. We explain the **GENERAL VIEWPOINT**. In other words, this is the way most people would explain the relationship problem.
3. We get **RADICAL**. We propose a new and different way of looking at the same problem. Some might shock you, and some might intrigue you. Either way, we hope to get you to think about your relationship complaints in a completely different way.

COMPLAINT 1

Adultery/Cheating

COMMON CAUSES: **1|** Fulfilling the need of closeness and/or sexual satisfaction, **2|** Easing mental pain that may or may not relate to the marriage, **3|** "Jolting" the partner into awareness of his or her pain, **4|** Repressing anger can surface as sex with someone else, **5|** overloaded by life's pressures, reaching out to others, **6|** experiencing emotional starvation, **7|** loving their partner, but are no longer "in-love," **8|** succumbing to intense attraction to someone with matching sexual chemistry, **9|** taking an opportunity presented, **10|** indulging during a crisis, such as the death of a family member, etc. There are hundreds of potential reasons for an affair. The real reason may be a combination of factors that are not knowable without years of therapy. Perhaps, the real reason may have nothing to do with the aggrieved partner.

GENERAL VIEWPOINT: Adultery is voluntary sexual intercourse between a married person and a partner other than the lawful spouse. If a couple, straight or gay, is not married but in a committed relationship, the term "cheating" is more appropriate.

You or your partner, for some reason, had mental or physical sex with someone outside the union. Keep in mind that not all affairs are physical. Emotional intimacy, involving secrecy and deception, is considered by some to be cheating. Maybe finding the reason for the cheating is important to understanding and accepting what happened. Maybe not.

RADICAL VIEWPOINT: Adultery/Cheating means having sex with someone you are not in love with. You might even be married to them, but if you no longer love them, then sex together is adultery. On the flip side, sex with someone you love is not adultery.

COMPLAINT 2

Third-Party Distraction

(A "closeness" with another person who takes attention away from the relationship)

COMMON CAUSES: The same causes described in Complaint 1: Adultery/Cheating, apply here. Meeting other people via e-mail, internet chat rooms, and dating sites, often open the door to third-party relationships. The person in contact with someone else is expressing a need that is not being fulfilled in the relationship. It is time to communicate directly and honestly about unfulfilled expectations and unmet needs.

GENERAL VIEWPOINT: If your partner remains in contact with someone with whom they once had a sexual or emotional affair, they are breaking the trust between the two of you. Trust is the foundation of a solid relationship. With a third party contaminating the environment, they will be unable to fully commit to your union. Commitment is the essence of love.

Deceptive behavior of this kind means your partner is going to be emotionally unavailable to you. They are distracted, feeding energy to another person, which, over time, may strengthen the outside union. Conflicting intentions will eventually generate a splintered personality, resulting in stress and emotional pain for the person who is not being honest about what they are doing. Even if they are not fully aware of their intentions, their predominant desire will eventually win out.

RADICAL VIEWPOINT: To unconditionally love another person, is to give them the freedom to be who they are without expectations, judgment, blaming or attempting to control their actions or reactions. You expect no more than your lover can give. You love them without expecting to them to change. In a union of unconditional love, your love is not dependent upon being loved in return.

COMPLAINT 3
Sexual Incompatibility

COMMON CAUSES: Although people experience different levels of biological desire at different times in their lives, other factors commonly inhibit sexual expression. If a person is overly passive toward the decision making of their partner, this will often generate a loss of desire in the partner. Emotional starvation, hidden resentments, and other forms of repressed pain will also reduce desire. Some people are underdeveloped sexually. Perimenopause or menopause can alter levels of desire. Feelings of responsibility, goal-orientation and anxiety will also suppress the sex drive. If none of these factors are valid, arousal is more likely when your partner is in a receptive state and they have freedom of choice.

GENERAL VIEWPOINT: You either want more sex or less sex than you are experiencing feeling deprived because your needs are not being honored, or resentful that your partner perceives your body as an object. If you want more sex, or more passionate sex, or kinkier sex, and your partner is turning a deaf ear to your needs, you may also feel you're being emotionally starved.

RADICAL VIEWPOINT: Sex is raw energy as well as one of the most important aspects of your life. If you try to repress your level of sexual desire to balance with a partner who has less desire, you will repress other aspects of your life such as creativity. When your sex life is flowing joyously, your life, your creativity, and all you do flows joyously. The partner with more desire needs to be free to establish other means of gratification. The person with less desire may need to assist their partner in establishing other avenues for sexual expression.

COMPLAINT 4
Financial Disagreement/ Hardship

COMMON CAUSES: While living beyond your means is the primary reason for financial problems, hardship is also caused by a job loss, an accident, or illness. Disagreement as to how money is spent indicates incompatible goals and values. If one of you wants to spend money on an exotic vacation and the other on a new car, compromise is in order. Also, when there isn't a clear understanding as to the responsibility of both people, agreements are in order. Who will pay what bills? Does the money go into a joint account or do you maintain separate accounts? The mechanics of fiscal management are not as important as a shared attitude about money.

GENERAL VIEWPOINT: Money problems are considered the second primary reason couples divorce. If you are in conflict with your partner about how money is earned, spent, or saved you are not alone. It is a subject you cannot avoid because it is so much a part of daily life. How money will be spent must be discussed and agreed to by both partners, so communication is a critical factor. Short-term and long-term goals need to be established and stuck to.

RADICAL VIEWPOINT: The more you can live in the ever-present NOW, the less you will be concerned with money. When you worry about money, you are living in the future. But there is no denying money is needed in our society for it buys us the freedom to choose the freedom to have more experiences. But as useful as money is, never allow yourself to be used by it, or allow it to become your master.

COMPLAINT 5
In-Law Interference

COMMON CAUSES: One partner may be more reliant on his/her parents than the other, or they may have been programmed to avoid conflict with Mommy and Daddy at all costs. If this is the case, the other partner will likely balk at in-law input. Both partners come from a different family background with different parental personalities as well as different values, expectations, and traditions. Parents think they know what is best for their children, and when they don't have natural boundaries, conflicts are assured.

GENERAL VIEWPOINT: Meddling, hovering, smothering in-laws are a major cause of marital conflict. Marriage counselors agree that three-quarters of all couples have in-law problems. One source of marital statistics says in-laws are the seventh primary cause of divorce. Obviously, it is better to keep in-laws out of your life, because they can cause resentment and serious problems. Outside interference will not help resolve a conflict. Even the Bible advises, "Therefore, shall a man leave his father and his mother and shall cleave unto his wife. And they shall be one flesh."

RADICAL VIEWPOINT: Adam and Eve got along well because neither had any in-laws to concern them. But for the rest of us, in-laws are what is. You're not going to change them, you need to alter how you view them. In most situations we don't actually solve problems, except through our viewpoint. By changing your viewpoint you can eliminate the effects of a problem, so you are no longer affected. If you're no longer affected by a problem you don't have a problem, although nothing about the problem situation may have changed.

COMPLAINT 6
Blended Families

COMMON CAUSES: **1**| The ex-spouse programs the children in negative ways toward you, **2**| The children view your marriage as a threat to the fantasy of getting mom and dad back together and feel that by sabotaging you that possibility exists, **3**| The children feel that by embracing you they are being disloyal to their other parent, **4**| If the parent died, the child will have idealized the former spouse and will feel guilty for embracing you.

GENERAL VIEWPOINT: Love for your partner will not resolve in-law problems. If you're the step-parent, it is not realistic to expect the children to like you, much less love you. They may never like you. Know too that their dislike is not personal. They would feel the same way about anyone in your position. Accept that the biological parent may not take your side when it comes to conflicts. It is not unusual for a step-parent to feel resentment, jealousy, indifference, anxiety, and even dislike for their step kids. The adult in the situation needs to act like an adult and avoid sinking to the children's level. If the problem is, after you married, the biological parent faded into the background and expected you to take over the parental role, you have a different problem that must be resolved by being direct and honest about your needs and desires.

RADICAL VIEWPOINT: Put your marriage before the demands of the children, but expect the children to come first when the parental parent is with their kids during visitation periods. If the children live with you and are manipulative, we're back to putting your marriage first.

COMPLAINT 7

Not Enough Time Together

COMMON CAUSES: **1|** You cannot change what you do not recognize and all too often spouses don't realize that they have become passing ships in the night, **2|** The pace of modern society takes up so much time there is none left for marriage, **3|** One of the spouses desires to spend separate time with friends or family, **4|** One partner desires more alone time than the other, **5|** The relationship is a low priority for one or both partners.

GENERAL VIEWPOINT: If you want to maintain a relationship, you must find ways to balance kamikaze schedules. The spouse who is busiest or most drained is the one who will determine how much time a couple has for each other. If that person has only a few moments a day for togetherness, that's all the "couple time" to be shared. Marriage must be made a priority if it is to survive. When you don't have enough time together to make love and have quiet conversations, disagreements and irritability take up more time than they did back in the days when you had time. But, if the spouse desiring more time together demands it, he or she may end up driving their partner away. "Time is the air love needs to breathe," says Mira Kirshenbaum in her book, *The Weekend Marriage.*

RADICAL VIEWPOINT: There is no longer enough time for marriage. In our fast-forward society, the loving connection between couples is all too often neglected in a rush of work, social obligations, problem solving, career building, children, commuting, e-mail, family needs, and household duties.

COMPLAINT 8
Immaturity/Selfishness/ Lack of Ambition

COMMON CAUSES: To be selfish, immature, or lack ambition might be explained as in-born personality traits. However, more often than not, how a person was raised has much to do with how they turned out. We are all programmed by early experiences, and if in growing up, your spouse was treated like a princess or a little lord, they may reflect and expect the same considerations as an adult. Keep in mind that people have a choice of being rationally or irrationally selfish. Irrational selfishness is what causes us to cringe at the word. But rational selfishness means one responds to the needs of others to obtain his/her objectives. You need to give to receive in human relationships.

GENERAL VIEWPOINT: Differing levels of maturity, selflessness, and ambition can generate relationship problems. One spouse may be career and goal-oriented, while the other is happy to work as little as possible. One may lie around all day and have no problem letting their partner do all the house work and/or take care of the children. One may be organized and like to plan their daily activities, while the other prefers to be "spontaneous" and unplanned. The resulting conflicts will require adult resolution skills.

RADICAL VIEWPOINT: In response to someone who is immature, selfish and/or lacks ambition, you want to yell, "GROW UP!" These are traits of spoiled, inconsiderate, infantile adults. Get over it, or get out.

COMPLAINT 9

Failed Expectations or Unmet Needs

COMMON CAUSES: Expectations and needs can be a tricky. A couple may start off fulfilling each other's needs, but with the passage of time and complications of life, maybe one partner begins to let things slide. The other partner feels their desires are unimportant and resentment ensues. A couple must make time to intimately communicate or the relationship will begin to be dysfunctional. Displaced resentments will generate conflicts over control and respect. As time passes, the couple will become hypersensitive, and angry responses can be expected in response to small issues. Without at least two hours of intimate focused conversation every week, the relationship cannot be expected to heal.

GENERAL VIEWPOINT: In a bonded relationship both partners must be direct and honest about their expectations and needs. Both have a right to receive loving consideration from their mate. Everyone needs to feel important to their partner and to receive emotional support. They need to feel loved for their hopes, dreams and desires as well as for their tangible contributions to the relationship. From a self-actualized perspective, expectations are considered futile, and we should learn to live without them. But realistically, when two people come together in love, and if their expectations and needs are reasonable and have been discussed and agreed to, both partners have an obligation to fulfill them.

RADICAL VIEWPOINT: If you want something out of your relationship, the problem is "wanting something." The less wanting in a relationship, the stronger it will be. When you insist that someone act according to your rules, they are forced to repress who they really are. Since long-term repression is impossible, any forced change will not last, assuring further disappointments.

COMPLAINT 10
No Fun or Romance

COMMON CAUSES: Although fun and romance are two different things, when they fade out of a relationship it is probably because of one or more of the other 23 complaints listed in this book. As examples, if there has been adultery, or there is a third-party distraction, or you experience sexual incompatibility, you are probably experiencing no fun or romance ... and these are just the first three complaints in this book. If one of you is emotionally drained or become hypersensitive to each other, there is little room left in your lives for romance. Fun and romance are critical to a good relationship—bring them back into your life by dealing with the key causes and check out the repairs we suggest below.

GENERAL VIEWPOINT: Fun and romance don't just happen by themselves. Both partners have to work at it. Each spouse knows what their partner enjoys and vice versa. The idea is to take a step in and initiate. Communicate. Both partners are responsible for romantic time. First, make the time for romance. Second, be creative. If one spouse is not willing to make the effort, there are plenty of potential people waiting in the wings who might like the opportunity to show their mate some fun and offer romance..

RADICAL VIEWPOINT: Neither partner should have to play the role of entertainment and intimacy coordinator. If one spouse feels they're not having enough fun or romance, they're the one who needs to initiate jointly enjoyed activities.

COMPLAINT 11

Poor Communication

COMMON CAUSES: Maybe one person wants to avoid disagreements, it is safer to remain quiet. Maybe one is uncomfortable about agreeing to a solution. Some people like locked-in agreements while others like to avoid rules and keep their options open. Consider that men and women usually communicate differently. Women tend to want their feelings acknowledged, while men tend to want to directly resolve problems. If one partner is doing something the other does not like, this needs to be addressed. The partner who is bothered needs to explain why they're having a problem with their partners actions or reactions. These needs should be expressed in a normal tone of voice, without being demeaning or accusatory.

GENERAL VIEWPOINT: Your partner refuses to communicate with you or they do not allow you to communicate directly and honestly about your wants and needs. Poor communication is often the root of other relationship problems. Neither partner can read the other's mind, without communication there is little hope of a harmonious relationship. Without communicating, you cannot make fair and balanced agreements about what does and does not work for both of you.

RADICAL VIEWPOINT: The primary reason two people who love each other cannot understand each other or get along is because of the past. When communicating, they're both interpreting through the past going over the past, digging though past hurts, past blame, past disappointments, unmet expectations and unmet needs. Instead, focus upon the present. Stay in the present. Express your present wants and needs as if the past did not exist.

COMPLAINT 12
Control Issues

COMMON CAUSES: Psychological studies claim that no matter how self-assured controllers appear to be, they're driven by feelings of vulnerability and lack self-esteem. On some level, they view their actions as being for their own protection. They may fear losing control altogether. No one likes uncertainty and in order to feel secure, we attempt to maintain the status quo through control. By doing this, the controller thinks their world will remain safe, and as a result, they will be happier. But, needing control actually expresses how inadequate the person feels about him/herself.

GENERAL VIEWPOINT: Controllers tend to be perfectionist, critical, demanding, rigid, and obsessive. Depending upon your association, they may have little respect for your privacy, and they are likely to be obsessed with particular issues. They seem to be incapable of withholding their opinion when encountering something they don't like. Opposition, even logical, warranted opposition, will send them sulking. They're probably Type A personalities to begin with.

When a spouse attempts to control with contemptuous remarks they have crossed a line that may lead to the end of the union according to many relationship counselors. Contempt is considered the most dangerous of the four relationship killers.

RADICAL VIEWPOINT: The four primary relationship killers are **1**| contempt, **2**| criticism, **3**| defensiveness, and **4**| withdrawal. All four are attempts to control your mate. Most relationship problems boil down to one person trying to control the other. Most of the conflicts in your life are the result of trying to control situations. But in reality, it is impossible to control another person.

COMPLAINT 13
Shared Responsibility Issues

COMMON CAUSES: Laziness and resentment are at the top of the list. After spending a day in the office, one partner resents coming home to take out the trash, and bathe the baby. So they let the trash accumulate in the kitchen, generating resentment from their partner. If one partner has the responsibility to change the oil in both cars, they may procrastinate out of laziness. They don't want to spend their Saturday afternoon at Jiffy Lube, so they watch a football game instead. Of course, one partner can forget, or outside responsibilities can keep them from fulfilling their commitments. If a couple can be flexible enough to pick up each other's slack once in awhile, life will be easier.

GENERAL VIEWPOINT: People need to be equal partners when it comes to assigning responsibility, and, initially, everything needs to be open to negotiation. When couples set up household and child-care responsibility chores so that one person is a subservient "helper" and the other has the authority and responsibility, the lesser partner has no ownership of the chore responsibility. Thus they are set-up to disappoint the key partner. All chores should be listed, and the partners can trade the unwanted ones. Each partner takes on their share. If one partner forgets or avoids a chore, the other should refrain from reminding them. Allow them time to be accountable on their own.

RADICAL VIEWPOINT: To be responsible means to be alert, conscious, mindful, and to act with awareness. Shared responsibility is a matter of cause and effect - what you give, you get back. If you disregard your share of the responsibility, you will receive a resentful response in return.

COMPLAINT 14
Addictions & Substance Abuse

COMMON CAUSES: If an addiction is not the result of depression or emotional problems nor substance based, counselors consider the concept of an "addictive personality." This is a distinct psychological trait that predisposes a person to compulsively behave in ways that their partner considers detrimental. They will often conceal the extent of their addiction and lie to cover themselves. They are usually immune to logical arguments to correct the situation. If your partner is addicted to the degree it is harming your relationship, you will most likely need professional help.

GENERAL VIEWPOINT: Addiction is usually considered a reliance on a substance or behavior that an individual has little power to resist. Some damaging addictions such as alcoholism can often be traced to symptoms of depression or emotional distress. It is easiest to explain substance-based addictions, including alcohol, cigarettes, drugs and prescriptions, which cause surges of dopamine in the brain that result in the user wanting to repeat the experience. Common behavioral addictions include gambling, shopping, eating, sex, work, and fervent attachment to a religion or a cause..

RADICAL VIEWPOINT: Everyone is addicted to something that "runs" them. The addiction concerning you may not be one of the heavy-duty cravings discussed below, but people can be addicted to negative thoughts and the feelings they generate. A common but rarely recognized addiction is conforming to society's idea of normalcy. Explore your own addictions before pointing your finger at others.

COMPLAINT 15
Incompatible Friends

COMMON CAUSES: 1| A long-standing relationship that originated in childhood may bring out the "immature child" in your partner, **2|** Different interests some people like to drink and party, while others are home-body types **3|** Senses of humor can vary. Maybe your partner and his/her friends have adopted a way of looking at the world that you just don't understand, **4|** Feeling excluded from your partner's "group" can cause problems. You may feel like an "outsider," **5|** Your partner may become selfish when he/she is around friends. They may ignore you in favor of socializing. **6|** One of you feels jealous or possessive of the other getting attention.

GENERAL VIEWPOINT: Personalities change in the presence of different people. If your partner says he/she does not like your friends, the problem may be the way you act when you're around them. While you might think your partner is being unreasonable, it may be that you become unlikable in the presence of these people. Or if it is you that does not like your partner's friends, reverse this situation. Just because we choose to enter a romantic relationship doesn't mean that everyone will automatically get along. All too often a spouse will choose to either fight about this problem and/or ignore their partner's friends. Neither strategy is productive.

RADICAL VIEWPOINT: You and you alone should be free to pick your social friends. But if your spouse doesn't like them, he or she should not have to be subjected to them. See them on your own. Ideally, you pick responsible friends who do not drive a wedge between you and your partner.

COMPLAINT 16
Lack of Emotional Support

COMMON CAUSES: One or both partners feel turned off toward the other. Maybe one of you felt neglected or felt that your desires were not important. Maybe you did not take the necessary time required to maintain a well-oiled relationship, or one of you withdrew from intimacy. Resentments built up over time cause you to become hypersensitive to each other and result in emotional pain, which then lead toward a downward spiral of mental detachment.

GENERAL VIEWPOINT: Emotional support means you feel that your partner is backing you up supporting you no matter what. This does not mean you agree with each other on everything, but it means treating your spouse in ways that project your love, trust and commitment to the marriage. It means you support your partner's differences without insisting they meet your needs in a specific way you want them met.

Examples of emotional support: spending free time with your mate, being open and honest about communications, paying attention to your mate's needs and concerns, sharing home responsibilities, giving occasional flowers, sharing personal experiences, and saying such phrases as: "I love you." "I'm proud of you." "I love being married to you." and "I'll be there for you."

RADICAL VIEWPOINT: We are evolving toward a level of awareness in which we will be "in the world but not of it," self-contained open to enjoying the all the warmth and joy life has to offer, but above the need of emotional support. If we have support, that will be wonderful. If we do not have support, that will be perfectly all right. It would not change what we felt or how we reacted to our mate. Most of us are far from having attained this enlightened level, but it is worth considering as a goal.

COMPLAINT 17
Constant Arguing

COMMON CAUSES: We are like robots. A robot has no choice in the way it acts. It has wiring and circuits and programmed to react according to its programming. Your mind operates the same way. When your buttons gets pushed by someone accusing you, challenging you, or blocking you, you demonstrate your machine-ness by responding with "being right." Everyone is programmed to "be right," and the argument begins.

GENERAL VIEWPOINT: There is a potential for arguing to be productive, but, more often than not, it becomes disruptive and has the potential to dominate your life. Arguing doesn't necessarily destroy a marriage, because some couples argue all the time and still have good marriages. How you argue is important. Couples need to develop communication and problem-solving skills to resolve their differences instead of allowing a cycle of conflict (resisting, attacking, withdrawing from each other) to develop. Ideally, both partners become 100% responsible for the state of the relationship. In other words, each person must become aware of their role in the conflict and take full responsibility for the loss of love.

RADICAL VIEWPOINT: A self-actualized relationship is one in which you accept your mate as they are, without judgment, expectations, blame, or trying to control. Arguing is an attempt to control your spouse—two people blaming each other or trying to tell the other what they want in a non-constructive way. When you blame your partner, you're saying that you're not responsible. You make yourself a victim, and blame becomes self-pity.

COMPLAINT 18
Lack of Commitment

COMMON CAUSES: Many people experience fear of commitment. The idea of forever makes them nervous. They equate commitment with loss of freedom/autonomy. Long-standing, unresolved issues between spouses are primary reasons one or both partners are not fully committed to each other. If your hearts are estranged and separated from one another, the union is weakened. Another common cause is not forgiving. One person is unwilling to forgive the other for something that happened or did not happen in the past.

GENERAL VIEWPOINT: Lack of commitment often means that one or both partners are unwilling to take the relationship to the next step. They may be so overwhelmed by life that they cannot focus on the union. Many factors can test the level of relationship commitment (child rearing, financial pressure, loss of a job, or physical illness) and challenge how committed one is to the union. It is commitment that holds two people together through difficult times.

RADICAL VIEWPOINT: If you're a workaholic, you are probably putting your career before your marriage. If you're trying to manipulate your mate into being the person you want them to be, you are not committed to a union of equals. If you spend many hours a day communicating with others on the internet and not spending one-to-one time with your spouse, you are not committed to your relationship. Any activity or absence used to avoid conversation and intimacy with your mate is an expression of non-commitment. Maybe it's time to ask yourself if you really want to be in a relationship.

COMPLAINT 19
Incompatible Goals & Values

COMMON CAUSES: Incompatible values and goals are often the result of a couple not communicating about this important subject prior to getting together. New opportunities, new people, and changing circumstances can also push this issue to forefront.

GENERAL VIEWPOINT: To fully grasp the concept of incompatible values and goals, rank your life-area priorities (values) in their order of importance, from one to ten. Key values are:

▪ Community/Political Involvement ▪ Finances ▪ Work/Career ▪ Friends/Associates ▪ Emotion/Love/Sex ▪ Spirituality ▪ Physical Fitness ▪ Family Life ▪ Education/Intellectual Development ▪ Creativity ▪ Recreation/Leisure Activities ▪ Physical Environment/Material Possessions.

Next list your ten most important goals. Decide which have the higher priorities by listing them from one to ten. Compare your values and goals. If your primary values are home and family, but your primary goal is to be your company's top road salesman, the goal and value are incompatible. You'll be on the road instead of at home enjoying your family.

RADICAL VIEWPOINT: An enlightened individual can adapt to any situation and will rise above the need to rank values and list goals, because unconditional love and peace of mind will be their only priorities. They will be patient, compassionate, and generous, and will have risen above the expectations of others. They know that the actions of other people does not affect them. Only what you think about what they do affects you.

COMPLAINT 20
Jealousy & Possessiveness

COMMON CAUSES: Fear drives jealousy and possessiveness. If someone considers their spouse to be his or her property, the idea that they might be lost leads to defensive and often aggressive behavior. Those who are jealous and possessive were often raised with high expectations and never learned to cope with limitations. They are insecure and feel inadequate. They compare themselves to others and find themselves lacking.

GENERAL VIEWPOINT: Awareness generates natural change. The person lacking trust, acting jealous, or being possessive needs to be aware that man suffers because of his craving to possess and keep impermanent things forever, such as his own person, loved ones, and material things. All things are impermanent, and as man tries to possess them, they slip away. As in trying to grasp water, the tighter you clutch, the faster it slips through your fingers. No one can possess another person, and no one can be possessed. Do not grasp at things that flow by in the stream of life. Instead, go with the flow of the current and become one with it and be aware that all things are simply waves in the water and trying to clutch them will only make them disappear. Jealousy and possessiveness destroy respect and trust in a relationship, which, in turn, destroy feelings of love and affection.

RADICAL VIEWPOINT: Those who are jealous and attempt to possess are themselves possessed. They are slaves to their own illusions about life. Possessiveness is a denial of the right of people and things to live and change. Thus, the possessor will push their partner away.

COMPLAINT 21
Lifestyle Differences

COMMON CAUSES: In the initial phases of a new relationship, we are like actors in a play trying to please the audience. But, you cannot repress who you are for long—to try is like standing upon a rubber raft in shallow water. As long as you stand on it, you can keep it submerged. In time, though, you will have to move on, and the raft will emerge. Your repressed emotions will emerge, and you be will become who you really are and do what you really want to do.

GENERAL VIEWPOINT: One of you likes to watch sports on TV in the living room every weekend. The other hates sports. One of you likes to attend the theater and cultural events. The other wants to go camping and watch stock car races. One of you likes to eat junk food, and the other gourmet. Classical music opposed to rock and roll. Romantic movies opposed to action flicks. One is social; the other, a social hermit. How did the two of you ever get together? We get together with partners who will test our patience and force us to grow by finding ways to co-exist and resolve problems in a win-win manner.

RADICAL VIEWPOINT: If your lifestyle differences force you to compromise to the degree you cannot become who you are meant to be, you are making a big mistake in allowing this to continue. You must learn to say "yes" when you want to say "yes," and "no" when you want to say "no." Being assertive is a matter of standing up for your human rights. Aggression is a matter of stepping upon someone else's human rights.

COMPLAINT 22
Abusive Behavior

COMMON CAUSES: The abuser may have a fear of abandonment and will resist anything in the partner's life that separates them, such as a job, family, friends, school, etc. People with Borderline Personality Disorders exhibit patterns of instability, impassivity, and behavioral swings between love and hate. Mood swings can also be triggered by poor diet and allergies. Other considerations include alcohol and drug abuse, depression, anxiety attacks, sleep disturbances, and disassociation. Perfectionist and domineering personalities tend to need to control. A rigid adherence to sexual roles can cause the male to attempt to dominate and control his world. Health problems and/or chronic illness can generate abusive behavior. Child abuse or parents who shame can set the stage for becoming an adult abuser. If a child witnessed or experienced battering, the experience can manifest as adult abusive behavior.

GENERAL VIEWPOINT: Abusive behavior includes all forms of verbal degradation, including expressions of contempt and disgust and uncontrolled anger. Jealousy, possessiveness, denial of powers, isolation, and threats can be abusive. Even stonewalling can be considered abusive. Couples in conflict tend to become ultra-sensitive to each other, which, over time, generates psychological warfare. This warfare increases over time. The partner being abused must not allow minor abuse to become major abuse. To do so will only legitimize the abuser's belief that he/she has a right to abuse. Psychopathic abusers have little or no conscience, and they are capable of displaying only shallow emotional responses.

RADICAL VIEWPOINT: Any attempt to manipulate another human being is abusive and should not be tolerated. Any physical abuse is an immediate reason to leave.

COMPLAINT 23
No Longer In-Love with Mate

COMMON CAUSES: There is a common downward spiral that causes people to fall out of love. Unfulfilled expectations and unmet needs generate resentment, which, in turn, generate conflicts that result in emotional pain, which causes a couple to become hypersensitive to each other. This destroys respect and trust, which results in dislike. The loss of feelings of love and affection are soon to follow.

In love, we don't want to feel pain. So, we try to control our relationship. We attempt to avoid rejection and avoid loss by controlling our partner. The need to control is a fear-based emotion, which pushes the other person away. No one can change someone else, nor can they expect another person to be anything other than who they are.

GENERAL VIEWPOINT: You want to feel passionately romantic toward your partner, but you do not. You go through the motions and probably live an outwardly acceptable life. For one reason or another, your partner has turned you off. Maybe for many reasons. Or, the situation may be in reverse, and your partner has turned off toward you.

RADICAL VIEWPOINT: Romantic love is a "scorchingly vivid turbulence" and "it is such a time-consuming, exhausting, ecstatic, painful, transforming business that it requires a long recovery in some cases, indeed, whole lifetimes," according to Dr. A C Grayling, an English philosopher. If after the passage of time, you are expecting to experience the same "scorchingly vivid turbulence" you did during the initial phase of your union, you are being unrealistic.

COMPLAINT 24
Your Mate "Changed"

COMMON CAUSES: Fear. We fear that we will lose something. There is only one problem that exists between human beings: fear. Fear is responsible for all disturbances, large or small, international, or interpersonal. Hatred, anger, possessiveness, tension, anxiety, greed, inhibition, stress, frustrations, hang-ups, phobias, insecurities, etc.—all are fear-based emotions. Upon accepting that the only problem between people is fear, we can simplify even more. There is only one fear: the fear of being unable to cope with a situation. You can cope with your partner's mid-life crisis, peri-menopause, menopause, illness, or financial setbacks.

GENERAL VIEWPOINT: When you resist change, your resist life. There is a Universal law that says, "What you resist, you draw to you." As long as you resist something, you are locked into it and perpetuate its influence in your life.
In *Callings*, Gregg LeVoy says, "We want to protect ourselves from change, because we're concerned with security. But more often than not the result is a reduction of our life-force. Our soul shivers and suffers. But we need to understand something about security. It isn't secure. The whole concept of security is contrary to the central fact that the life constantly changes. When we avoid change, we isolate ourselves from living."

Misery will arise out of our resistance.

RADICAL VIEWPOINT: If your mate did not change, he/she would become boring, and you would grow tired of their company. Hope and pray for your mate to change. Without change, you have stagnation, and your relationship is doomed. Life is change. Change is the only thing that is permanent.

COMPLAINT 25
Lack of Appreciation

COMMON CAUSES: On a human level, the cause of lack of appreciation is being self-centered. If another person does something nice for you but you do not say a simple "thank you," then you are being selfish and thus, not appreciative. However, on a spiritual level, perhaps the cause is deeper. It could be negative karma incurred from a past life. Or as discussed above, it may be simply a response to the vibration your partner is sending out to you.

GENERAL VIEWPOINT: Most people blame their partner for all the problems in their relationship. In other words, they have a difficult time admitting when they are wrong. They look at their behaviors and conclude that their partner does not appreciate them. If they could only "fix" the other person and make them less self-centered, then all would be well.

RADICAL VIEWPOINT: Lack of appreciation is really just another way of saying you are putting negative vibrations out into the world. According to scientists, the emotions that vibrate the fastest are love and appreciation. The ones that vibrate the slowest are any one that is based in fear (resentment, jealousy, anger, etc). You may think that your partner does not appreciate you, but it could be that you are creating the situation because of the vibrations you are contributing to the relationship.

SECTION TWO

Maintenance & Repair

Table of Contents

SECTION TWO TIPS FOR MAINTENANCE & REPAIR

Accepting What Is. 32
Negative-Minded Mate. 33
ACT!!. 34
Stop Your "Soap Operas" 35
Teach Your Partner How to Treat You 36
Imagine Your Partner's Death 37
You Do Not Have To Be In Control. 38
Be Right & Lose The Game 39
Re-Think "Trust" 40
Reframe Your Anger 41
Give Up Control. 42
Stop Being Possessive. 43
Invoke the Law of Experience 44
Selfishness 45
Bring the Meaning Back 46
Stop Being a "Victim" 47
Face Your Problems. 49
Take Therapy Seriously 50
Fear & Relationships. 51
Love & Attachment. 52
Take All The Blame 53
Have a Goal 54
Remove Your Masks 55
Habit vs. Love 56
Stop Codependency 57
Intermittent Reinforcement. 58
Role Play. 59
Happiness. 60
Happiness II 61
Youthful Energy 63
Comfort and Discomfort 64
Love vs. Scarcity 65
Equality 66
Don't Argue With Feelings. 67
Physical Conditions. 68
Accountability. 70
Increase Your Self-Discipline 71
Control Your Subpersonalities 72
Create Aliveness 73
Make the Right Choices. 74
Be Direct & Honest 75
Judging Others. 77
Four Ways to Vanquish Anger 78
Stress 79
Look in the "Mirror". 80
Don't Try to Change Your Partner. 81
Don't Take Things Personally 82
Be an Inspiration to Your Partner. 83
Become More Empathetic. 84
What You Deny to Your Partner Will be Denied to You 85
Totally Commit. 86
Control Yourself. 87
Strive for Unconditional Love 88
Do Little Things. 89
Live For Yourself, Not Your Partner. 90
Detached Mind. 91
Consider Your Ego 92
Anger as Manipulation 93
Relationships As A Busy Street 94
Respect & Reciprocity. 95

Sex is a Mirror 96
Make Making Love Special 97
Be Present 98
Perception is Reality 99
Stop! Rate the Vibrations 100
Take Psychological Responsibility 101
Autonomy vs. Connection 103
Women as "Relationship Experts" 105
Relationship Monitoring 107
Ingredients for Romance & Intimacy . . . 108
Interpersonal Power 110
Use the "Test of Publicity" 111

RADICAL TIPS FOR MAINTENANCE & REPAIR

Extramarital Affair Triangle 114
Uncover Past Life Ties to Your Partner . . . 115
Balance Your Male/ Female Energy Ratio 116
Sexual Morality? 117
Feng Shui Your House 118
Empaths 119
Release Sexual Pressure 120
Harness the Power of the Law of Attraction 121
Sex & The Law of Magnetism 122
Creative Visualization 123
Create Your Own Reality 124
Investigate Your Parallel Lives 125

This section is for people who are:

1. Currently in a relationship

or

2. Want a relationship and will probably be in one in the near future.

> **MAINTENANCE** You might be satisfied with your relationship, but you just want some tips for keeping it happy and healthy.
>
> **REPAIR** You might be on the brink of a break-up, and therefore, you need to tools for repair.

Either way, this section is for maintaining or re-creating a happy relationship.

Accepting What Is

Life on earth includes suffering. We have relationship problems. We lose loved ones through separation or death. We experience loneliness, sickness and accidents. We are haunted by guilt. We have monetary hardships. We experience phobias and fears and have unfulfilled desires.

We experience this distress because we desire things to be different than they are. In short, *it is your resistance to what is that causes your suffering.* When we say suffering, we mean everything in your life that does not work.

Some things are facts. Income taxes exist, and that is what is. Your partner is quiet and stubborn . . . that's what is. Your mate had an affair . . . that's what is. You can spend your life attempting to change what is, but there is not much you are going to do about it. Instead, concentrate your efforts upon things you can change.

Remember the Serenity Prayer: "God grant me the serenity to accept the things I cannot change, the courage to change the things I can, and the wisdom to know the difference."

You need to understand that it is impossible to change another human being. You may be in a position to force change with a statement like, "If you don't stop doing that, I'm going to leave." Your partner may stop, but they will be repressing their real emotions, and repression will always surface — often in even more undesirable forms.

You can change your attitude and the way you respond to your partner. As a result, your partner will be responding to a "new you," and they may change all on their own. You cannot expect to see long-term results from asking for or demanding a change.

When you accept what is, you simply accept logical facts — unalterable realities. Actually, you have no choice in accepting what is. It is what is. You have a choice in how you respond to what is.

Negative-Minded Mate

Is your partner dissatisfied, cynical, pessimistic, and /or sullen? Do they gripe, whine or put you down? Maybe they complain about what you have or have not done, or about their job, or the mess in the garage, or the state of the nation. A negative-minded person sees the glass as half-empty.

Let us begin with a statement echoed throughout this book: You cannot change your mate or lover. You can change yourself, and your partner may respond to the new you by changing, but don't count on it. People are who they are. Accept who they are and spend your energy finding ways to deal positively with who they are.

Be advised that it will seldom serve you to try to prove a pessimistic or negative person wrong. Respond to their negativity with a positive statement. Maybe your mate complains about how unhappy they are at work. You say, "I have confidence in you and your ability to find a better job if you decide that's best action to take."

The pessimist will probably respond, "The job market is terrible, and I can't take time off work to search for a new opportunity." You respond, "Where there's a will there's a way. I know how determined you can be when you really want something." Smile and refuse to be further sucked into the discussion. It will not serve you to try to be right.

When you are constantly confronted with negativity, it is only natural to become negative yourself—avoid falling into this trap. Don't let their negativity dictate how you act or react. Let your partner learn that you will not buy into their game; eventually they will get tired of playing. If your partner's attitude generates negative self-talk in your mind, counter this programming with your own positive affirmations.

ACT!!

Most people live a life of "good intentions." In other words, they are "all talk and no action." Are you one of those people? Do you constantly complain about the state of your relationship, but have not done anything about it?

If this sounds like you, you need to examine the reasons you don't take action. With no action, there can be no improvement. You can sit and wish your relationship to be better, but it won't make it happen. You need to commit to living a life of action.

There are two reasons most people don't take action. First, they are not really committed to making a change. They probably think they are, but, if they were, they would be doing something. I am sure that if a reliable psychic told you the winning numbers to tomorrow's lottery, you would not hesitate to take the action to go buy that ticket. You would be committed to winning the lottery because you want to. When we want something badly enough, most people do not hesitate to take action.

The other reason people do not take necessary action is because of fear. Most people fear change, though they claim they want it. Change requires taking risks. It requires moving out of your comfort zone to create a more desirable reality. Even though many people complain about their relationship, the actions that would be required to make the positive changes would take them out of their comfortable, predictable, familiar lifestyle.

You need to get clear on where you stand with change and fear. Are they holding you back from action? If so, are your fears valid? If your relationship stayed the way it is forever (or got worse), would that be better than taking an exciting risk to change it?

You must no longer tolerate the mindset of "non-action." It will get you and your relationship absolutely nowhere.

Stop Your "Soap Operas"

Television soap operas are over-dramatized and, in some cases, just downright ridiculous. They are created for entertainment. You must realize that you have most likely created many soap operas of your own that are not helping your relationship.

We all have soap operas. In other words, we have stories that we repeat in one form or another until we can verbalize them without thinking. They are tapes we play at every opportunity.

It is likely that everyone who is close to you knows your soap operas. They have heard them so often that they could probably repeat them word for word, just as you could repeat theirs. When you talk about them, it feels good to "vent" and get it "out." However, this is just a short-term "fix." In the long run, it is doing nothing to help the situation.

Here are some common relationship soap operas: "My husband doesn't pay any attention to me," "My wife doesn't give me enough sex," "He never helps me with the kids," or "She spends too much money." No matter what the topic, the repetition only programs your subconscious more to produce more of the same. If you want your soap opera to change, you must stop thinking and talking about it.

Instead of basing your relationship on negative soap operas, try creating some new ones. They may not be true yet, but the mere act of playing positive ones over and over in your head will actually create that outcome. Your subconscious doesn't know the difference between fantasy and reality. If it "hears" good things on a regular basis, it will start to "believe" it and automatically work towards that goal.

You are the person who manifests everything in your life, and if you focus on your negativity, you will never be able to move beyond it.

Teach Your Partner How to Treat You

Most people are not treated with the respect they deserve. Their partner may yell, scream, say nasty words, or call them names. This is unacceptable. Parents correct their children when they do such things, so why wouldn't you correct your partner?

If you are treated disrespectfully, why do you allow it? There has to be reason, or it would not be occurring. Let's turn the tables around and look at it from an objective standpoint. If one of your friends were receiving the treatment that you are, what would you say to him/her? Would you think it's acceptable? Probably not.

Most people speak before they think. They let their emotions rule and say things they may regret later. To avoid this, it is important to understand a vital principle of communication: it is irreversible. In other words, once you say something, it is "out there," and you can never take it back. You can try, but it won't work. You can say, "Oh, I didn't mean that. I just said it because I was angry." But, it doesn't matter. It is already said, and the damage to the relationship is already done.

Chances are, however, that your partner is not the only one who speaks before thinking. You probably do it too. One way to stop this behavior on both sides is to become aware of when it is happening. You must step back and say to your partner and yourself, "This is unacceptable behavior. We must require more of each other. We should treat each other with the utmost respect."

We teach people how to treat us. What are you teaching your partner? What negative behavior are you allowing? What negative behavior is your partner allowing from you? It all goes back to the old saying, "Do unto others as you would have done to you." Demand nothing but the same from them—you deserve it.

Imagine Your Partner's Death

Singer Tim McGraw sings a popular song called, "Live Like You Were Dying." It sends a powerful message to everyone listening: don't take anything for granted, especially your life. The song implies that you shouldn't wait until your days are numbered to really live.

You can apply this same philosophy to your relationship and your partner. Unfortunately, most people take others for granted. They don't think about the fact that their lives could change in the blink of an eye. The ones we love could be gone tomorrow. Intellectually and logically, they may understand it, but, emotionally, it doesn't usually enter their minds. It's "something that happens to other people," not to them. The funny thing is, if everyone thinks it happens only to other people, who does it really happen to?

For this repair, you can use the power of your imagination to see what life would be like without your partner. Here's a scenario you can use: Your partner has been complaining of chest pains for months. He is only 38, so neither of you are terribly worried. Time passes, and he frequently talks about making a doctor's appointment but never finds the time to get around to it. You both talk to others about the symptoms. One friend says it's because he just started an exercise program. Another says maybe it's a symptom of sleep apnea. But, neither of you took it seriously. Then, you get a call at work from your partner's boss. He dropped dead in the gym at work.

How would you feel? Do you think all of the complaining you did about him was worth it? When you find yourself playing negativity over and over in your head, stop yourself. Think about how this could be his final day on earth. How would you treat him? Probably not like you are doing right now.

You Do Not Have To Be In Control

We want to manipulate and control our circumstances, but these are fear-based emotions. We're here on earth to learn to let go of our fear-based emotions, such as prejudice, selfishness, jealousy, envy, blame, repression, greed, the desire to control, and the list goes on and on and on.

The need to manipulate and control is a big fear. If it applies to you, we suggest that you consider the fact you don't have to be in control to survive.

You can detach from the conflicts and confusion in your life by simply refusing to try to control the outcome. In the following process, ask yourself each question and listen for the first thought that comes up in response.

- Are you trying to control your partner's actions or reactions to you?
- Why? What do you fear might happen?
- What if that did happen? What is the worst it would mean for you?
- What if you were to integrate your fear by letting go and allowing circumstances to flow to their logical conclusion?
- Which is the growth choice?
- Can you give up your expectations? If the other person comes through, great; if they don't come through, that's okay too.

Usually, attempts to control are efforts to get someone else to change and become what you want them to. You can't change other people. It doesn't work. Even if you manage to get what you want, it won't last. The other person will be repressing who they are, and no one can do that for long.

In the case of severe conflicts, sometimes the only way to be responsible to yourself is to remove yourself from the environment you find yourself in. If you're going to stay around, what do you have to lose by just mentally standing over in the corner and observing?

Be Right & Lose The Game

Is your partner someone who thinks they are always right? No matter the situation, they are the final word? If so, you need to know that they were programmed to be exactly the way they are, and you can use the knowledge to your advantage.

Your subconscious mind is a memory bank and operates much like a computer. It's programmed for survival and for you to be "right." Everything you consider saying or doing is quickly run through your memory banks and compares the present to related past experiences. Your computer then approves your actions as compared to the past, because in the past you "survived."

To rise above this programming, learn to be aware of your programming so you can detach from the buttons that cause you to respond automatically. When your button is pushed, you need to be right. Even if you are not right, you will find some way to justify yourself. Only those with enlightened awareness of how human beings work will understand this. Let your partner be right. You want to win the game. Winning is far more satisfying than getting to be right.

Learn to override your own "rightness" button. Knowing how your partner is programmed to function, you can let him be right. Unless you allow him to be right, his survival is threatened, and there is going to be trouble. You can quickly allow him to be right with a phrase such as, "I understand how you feel," or, "I can certainly acknowledge your position on the matter." You are not admitting he is right, but you're taking him off 'tilt.' His survival will no longer be threatened, and he can concentrate upon the problem.

If you're being blamed for not doing something, say, "I realize I should have done that, but I didn't. What can we do about it?" Notice the "we." Bring your partner in to help resolve the situation.

Re-Think "Trust"

Trust is a big issue in many relationships. Perhaps one person cheated, and that has weakened the relationship. The cheated-on partner usually says, "I can't trust you anymore." If an affair never took place in the relationship, trust is still a problem for most couples. Perhaps, one of the partners was cheated on by another mate and has transferred distrust to their current partner. Maybe no cheating occurred, but they have a problem trusting people in general.

Whatever the reason, if you are the person struggling, it is best to look within yourself for answers. The fact that you don't trust your mate has little to do with your mate and has to do with two other reasons. The first reason is your perceived ability to deal with possible situations. For example, if you think, "I don't trust Bob, because I think he's going to cheat on me," what you are really worried about is your inability to cope with the situation if it should arise. You are stressing about a future event that may or may not happen. Meanwhile, you are not enjoying and living in the moment. As a result, you are robbing yourself of happiness.

The second reason you don't trust your mate is because of your sense of self-worth, which is intimately tied with how much you trust other people. If you think you are worthy of love, respect, and commitment, you will expect and receive nothing less. If you think you don't deserve any of those, your low expectations will inevitable create the reality you desperately want to avoid.

You need to realize that you can be strong and confident. You can deal with whatever life brings your way. You deserve a quality partner who will give you everything you desire. Don't settle for anything less.

Reframe Your Anger

When we get upset with someone, we usually let our anger loose. We act emotionally, not logically. We frequently speak before we think. This only works to our disadvantage.

Next time you get angry with your partner, reframe the situation. Think of it as a test that the Universe has given you. The reason we are all here on earth is to learn to express unconditional love. Most people are not capable of it. Some people can't even define it. But, that doesn't change the fact that we are learning how to do it.

Think of the Universe as your teacher. It gives you lessons; it gives you tests. The lessons occur in many forms. For example, you are reading this book right now and learning many things. It is one thing to read about them (you can even think you really understand it all), but, when it comes down to it, we don't know how well we've learned these lessons until we are tested. So, expect lots of tests in the form of relationship problems.

How do you usually respond to undesirable situations? Do you respond with anger and negativity? Or, do you respond with compassion or neutrality? Until you learn that negative, fear-based emotions don't work, you will be faced with similar situations until you "get it."

Remember that you got angry because you had expectations of approval or control. You wanted to gain approval of your partner or control their actions. Another idea that has been echoed throughout the book is: your expectations are in conflict with what is. It would be impossible for you to be angry if you didn't have any expectations.

Where do you get the right to expect your partner to be the way you want him/her to be? You wouldn't want them to expect you to live up to their expectations; don't expect them to either.

Give Up Control

There are many ways people try to control their partners. Some of the most common strategies people are: criticism, anger, guilt, insecurity, obligation, withholding, helplessness, teasing, and asking questions.

Some people may be very conscious and deliberate about their control. Perhaps a wife leaves her husband a list of chores to be done before he can go golfing with his friends. If he doesn't comply, she responds with anger. Others may be more subtle and not even be aware of their actions. This type of person may make insinuations about how chores need to be done and covertly withhold affection until it happens. Either way, trying to exert control on your partner does nothing but damage the relationship.

When you attempt to control and manipulate other people, you express fear and establish a very destructive climate in the relationship. You fear that your reality will not be the way you want. The wife who makes lists for her husband fears that her house will be messy, and she will be unable to cope. Perhaps, she fears that her husband will never clean the house unless she makes him. Whatever the fear, it is directly tied to your selfish way of looking at the world. You want your world to be the way you want it to be. Doesn't your partner deserve the same? The answer is yes to both of those questions. The tricky part is to figure out a good way to make everything acceptable to both parties.

Ask yourself: Am I controlling my partner? Is my partner controlling me? If so, what actions can I take to make the climate of our relationship more harmonious? The answer lies in giving up control. Don't control your partner and don't allow yourself to be controlled by him/her. Then, both of you will feel more free and loving toward the other person.

Stop Being Possessive

When people enter into a committed relationship, both partners think they assume "ownership" of the other person. This is called possessiveness. Most people don't think anything of it; it seems completely natural and logical to be possessive of your mate. However, you must realize that it is very destructive to a relationship.

No one really "owns" anyone else. In fact, there aren't many things in life that we do "own." Even if you "own" a house or a car, unless you have paid the bank in full, you are not the owner—the bank is. Therefore, as you can see, ownership is usually an illusion. Either it doesn't exist, or it's temporary.

For example, you may think you "own" your children. While they may be your responsibility for 18 years, you do not possess them. They are their own person, and they will eventually grow up and leave. Even if you perceive this as a type of ownership, it really isn't. "Possessing" them is only temporary.

Possession is the ultimate expression of insecurity. Those who are most guilty of this emotion are the ones who think they will never have enough. In relationships, that usually means not having enough love, attention, or affection. People only want possession because they feel something is missing or lacking. This usually leads to grasping tighter in order to make sure that nothing else is lost.

The person who is being "possessed" will usually experience a paradox. They may feel complimented and loved because of their partner's presumed ownership, but they may desire to be free.

Possessiveness is fear. If you require "ownership" of your partner, what is your real fear? What needs do you have that are not being met? What actions of yours are causing you to have a disharmonious relationship? You must think about these things or else this fear will take over and ultimately destroy the relationship.

Invoke the Law of Experience

The information that our brain collects from our experiences remains there unless new information is entered. If that happens, our minds will be re-programmed. Every situation we encounter has the potential to override old information and create new experiences.

Let's take an example. When you first met, your experience of your partner was probably joyous and loving. In the infatuation stage, we think there is nothing wrong with the other person; they are perfect. However, as time goes on, we see the things our partner does and, eventually, they start to irritate us in one way or another. Thus, the original information of them being perfect is re-programmed. Now, we think they are less-than-perfect. In fact, sometimes we find them downright annoying.

If your relationship has been damaged by negative information that has overridden the positive, you need to do something about it. You need to invoke the Law of Experience. You need to create fresh, new input to erase the trauma of the past.

You can accomplish this through a number of ways. You can attempt to change your energy (see Repair #00), inspire change in your partner (see Repair #00), use mind-programming techniques, or simply harness the power of your creative imagination.

The easiest way to do it is by using your imagination. All you need to do is put some effort into visualizing how you want your partner to be. It has been determined that the subconscious mind does not know the difference between fantasy and reality. This works to your advantage, because the more you see your relationship as you want it to be, the more your subconscious thinks that is actually your real experience. Eventually, your mind will accept this reality and invoke the Law of Experience. You will ultimately overcome old fearful programming with exciting, positive images.

Selfishness

Are you selfish? You probably don't think you are, but maybe you should go ask your partner. His/her opinion matters more than yours when it comes to the relationship.

Everyone is selfish on some level because it is biologically programmed every human being. Before we had modern civilization, the cave-men (and women) had to be selfish to survive. They were hunting prey for food and fighting off animals so they wouldn't be eaten alive. They were also competing with each other. If they didn't get their fair share of the food, they would die. If they were loving and let everyone else in the tribe eat their food, they would starve. So, selfishness is really a survival mechanism, which isn't necessarily a bad thing. If we weren't wired that way, the human race would have died out a long time ago.

This mentality used to serve a purpose. The problem is that many people in our civilization don't need to be selfish to survive anymore. Nonetheless, this mindset still exists, and it prevents happy relationships. We are programmed to be selfish for survival reasons, but then it spills over and manifests into behaviors, such as wanting time to sit on the couch and neglect your partner or a myriad of other things that complicate relationships.

Strive for balance. Know your own needs and get them met. You also have the responsibility to discover what your partner's needs are and meet those as well. Both partners really need to be equally concerned with the other's happiness. It's hard to be unselfish if your partner is always selfish. When someone never meets your needs, you really don't want to meet theirs either. It makes you almost bitter because your needs are being neglected by that other person.

Turn the tables on yourself. Assess your level of selfishness and how that is damaging your relationship. Then, change it.

Bring the Meaning Back

One of the benefits of having special people in our lives is to give us meaning. This is not to say that we shouldn't have our own meaning outside of relationships (within ourselves), but the people who are close to us should add to our lives and not subtract from it.

Everyone needs a purpose, a meaning, or a reason to live. A good analogy is when someone retires. Frequently, their health deteriorates, and they are not as vibrant as they were when they were working. That is because their purpose, their meaning is gone. They have "no reason to get up in the morning."

The same is true for relationships. When you first met, there were probably extreme levels of meaning. The roses were a richer red, and everything in life looked sweeter — that is the feeling that manifests from having a purpose.

Unfortunately, after a couple is together for a while, this meaning seems to evaporate. You no longer look forward to that "once-a-week" date or simply holding their hand and cuddling up to them. Those little things that meant so much to you in the beginning have disappeared. Unlike retirement, when relationships go through this, there is no clear "event" to mark the changes. Instead, we notice them, mourn the loss of them, and do nothing about them.

If your memories of how your relationship used to be exceed how things are (or could be with some effort), you have a serious problem. You can't live in the past or the future. All you have is now. You cannot live without positive, meaningful challenges that propel you into the future.

You need to figure out what will give your relationship more meaning. You need bring some little things back. Without it, your relationship is destined to end.

Stop Being a "Victim"

There is no such thing as a victim. Instead, there are people who choose to play the victim role. This concept is particularly applicable to relationships, because most people think they are the victim of the other person's actions. Let's take a look as some qualities of a "victim" so you can see if you fit into this category:

- They believe they don't have any power.
- They always blame others for anything that happens to them.
- They are addicted to pain and fear.
- They have very little joy in their lives/relationship.
- They take very little responsibility for their feelings.
- They feel at the mercy of others.
- They judge others.
- They thrive on drama.

We create our own reality. If you are playing the victim role, you will only have negative emotions, which will create negative experiences. You can choose to stop being a "victim." When you make that choice, your life and relationship will become better. You will feel more positive and light. You will "take back" your power.

- Try to become a master of your own relationship and life. When you do this, you will see the following characteristics start to form within yourself:
- Non-judgmental
- Joyful
- Peaceful and calm
- Powerful
- Blame no one but yourself
- No regrets about anything

Masters act. They don't react. Acting means being centered and taking control of your circumstances. You no longer allow other people to dictate how you feel or what your life is like.

You need to take some time to seriously consider your "victim" status. Decide right here and now that you will no longer play that game. Take back the power and watch your relationship improve.

Face Your Problems

When a relationship hits troubled waters, sometimes both people like to put their heads in the sand and try to ignore it. They pretend it isn't happening because it is too risky to address the problems. However, it is better to face a fearful situation than to avoid it.

Many people don't like conflict and will go to great lengths to avoid it. For example, maybe both partners grew up in a household where their parents fought constantly. As children, that made them fearful, so, as adults, they made the decision (either separate or together) to avoid confrontation at all costs. While they had good intentions, all it did was sweep the problems under the rug where they fester and get worse. Avoiding negative issues doesn't make your relationship more peaceful; it ultimately destroys it.

You need to accept that whenever two people get together, conflict is inevitable. That's what is. Neither will see reality from the same exact viewpoint—ever. Once you realize this, you can begin to visualize how you will face and deal with the fearful situations.

Don't use fear as a justification for avoiding joy in your relationship. Don't live by the ridiculous motto of "don't fix it if it ain't broke." Anyone who lives like that is just making excuses for not putting effort into their relationship. If you do, it creates subconscious programming, and you could actually program yourself to fear losing your fear. To give up your pain would mean taking away something from you. As crazy as it sounds, most people are "addicted" to their pain and personal problems. It gives them a sense of identity—even if it's not a positive one.

You need to decide to stop avoiding your problems. Face the fear. Make the effort. Throw away the addiction to pain. Then, and only then, will you be living up to your ultimate potential.

Take Therapy Seriously

When a couple has problems, it is natural to think about seeing a marriage counselor. In theory, this is a great idea. An objective third party can help you re-frame your problems and become more sensitive to your partner's needs. If it is taken seriously, therapy will help. If not, it won't.

Let us repeat: therapy will not work if it is not taken seriously. There are countless couples in the world who go, listen to the counselor talk, and then after a few short weeks or months, they stop. This may be a deliberate decision or it might be that "life" gets in the way of attending on a regular basis.

There are two important things you need to know about therapy. Not only do you need to show up and listen, you also have to act. Simply sitting on the psychologist's couch does not repair a marriage. It requires action on both people's parts. For example, if the therapist says to do something romantic for your partner that week, do it! Don't sit around and wonder if your mate will do it first. Just do it! Leave him a card or a note to meet you in the bathroom at 9:00 p.m. Have a bubble bath, candles, and wine waiting for him. Make the best of it. If your partner is the one who does it first, you need to reciprocate or else your partner will stop trying.

Some people never even make it to therapy. They think they are too good for it or they will be "blamed" for everything in the relationship. If you fall into any of those categories, we have a message for you: grow up. You are an adult who has a responsibility to yourself and others.

Therapy can be a great experience. But, you need to have the right attitude and mindset before you go.

Fear & Relationships

Most relationships have jealousy and possessiveness. It seems like those emotions are rooted in love; we are jealous that our partner might fall for someone else because we love them, and, therefore, we are possessive. But, even though it "looks" like love, it isn't. It's fear.

These emotions are the manifestation of insecurity, which, in essence, is fear. If you are jealous or possessive, it is because you think you are not "good enough." If you were totally confident and able to express unconditional love, you would believe that your partner need not find anyone else but you. You are worthy of his love. In fact, he/she is probably lucky to have you.

Unfortunately, many people are not capable of feeling and acting this way. Instead, they feel that to be important, they must "possess" their partner. The way that is usually accomplished is through attempting to control their behavior. For example, if your mate has recently become friends with a woman at work, don't ask dozens of questions about her. Don't ask where he's been, if he's seen her, or what she looks like. All of these questions appear to be merely inquisitive, but they are really just a covert way of saying, "I know you're friends with a woman. I don't like it. I want you to know that I know I don't like it. I want you to affirm to me that you love me and only me."

When others attempt to control our behavior, the response is usually rebellion. No one likes to be controlled. No one likes to be around insecure people. It becomes annoying and emotionally draining. If you think you fall into this category (a person who expresses fear and insecurity in their relationship), try to analyze your fears. You will probably find them unfounded. Once you do, you can move past them and towards unconditional love.

Love & Attachment

Most love is conditional, "I will love you if you are willing to be what I want you to be and do what I want you to do!" But, conditional love is attachment. Attachment is bondage. If the love you share with your partner is bondage, it is also an illusion.

A self-actualized love of unconditional acceptance will not become attachment. The moment you say to your partner, "Love only me," you are attempting to possess them. In possessing, you are making your lover into an object — a thing — something to be used.

According to philosopher Immuanel Kant, to treat another person as a means is an immoral act. In other words, if you see your lover as being there for your gratification, or to fulfill your sexual desires, or to provide something else for you, you are reducing your partner to an object. Thus, you are in bondage to each other.

Once you are in bondage, you will desire freedom again. Whatever you get, you will become bored with it, and whatever you desire but do not get, you will long for. If you desire freedom while trying to possess your partner, a struggle is assured. In trying to possess your partner, you will end up being possessed by your partner.

The solution is to become self-actualized. A self-actualized individual will have risen above the need to control others. He or she expresses no blame, no expectations, and no negative judgments. They will be well on their way to developing detached mind — a level of awareness in which they mentally fluctuate only from positive to neutral as outside conditions change. In other words, they allow negativity to flow through them without affecting them. Self-actualization and unconditional love are much the same. On the surface, they both feel a little like indifference, but they amount to accepting someone else for what they are and not expecting them to change to be who you want them to be.

Take All The Blame

From a human-potential perspective: Blame is self-pity.

From a karmic perspective: Blame is incompatible with karma and reincarnation. How can you blame someone for helping to teach you the lesson you were incarnated to learn? Both parties were acting out their karma.

In the book, *How Loving Relationships Work*, therapist Anne Geraghty says, "The one that apparently initiates a change in the dynamics/agreements of the relationship or lifestyle may not be the one that has really instigated it."

With that in mind, how can you begin to assign blame? When two people are having problems, both are responsible. You might be in therapy ten years and never uncover the deep churnings beneath the behaviors.

From an astrological perspective, let's say you're a couple. One of you had an affair, which generated a major crisis in your marriage. A good astrologer will be able to pinpoint the situation in both your charts. If it's in both charts, it was destined to be experienced by both of you as a learning opportunity.

Life in the physical body is about making growth choices and experiencing the consequences of your actions through cause and effect. Ideally, you learn through love and wisdom. If not, there's the old reliable teacher — pain. Suffering makes a point and you learn, but only if you let go of the blame.

All things considered, why not accept ALL THE BLAME. After all, you're karmically responsible anyway, and it will end the arguing.

We're all working toward enlightenment. Self-actualization is a step in the right direction, and it amounts to letting go of the fear-based emotions and learning to express unconditional love — unconditional acceptance. In other words, accept others without expectations, blame, judgment, or trying to control. I know, I know — you've heard it before.

Have a Goal

If you want to succeed in life, you have to have a goal. You can't get to where you want to be unless you know how to get there. For example, you would never think to set off on vacation without some sort of plan. You would never just pack your bags, get into your car, and say, "Okay, let's go on vacation" without knowing where it was you were going.

Relationships are no different than a vacation. You can't get to where you're going if you don't know where you want to go. You can't say, "I wish my relationship was better" and expect it to happen magically. You have to clearly see your goal and your destination. It's not easy. Most people aren't clear on their destination, and, therefore, they wander aimlessly hoping the wind will carry them to it. But, the wind will probably only carry you to places you don't want to be.

If you do know where you want to go, you need to plan how to get there. As an analogy, let's say you live in Lincoln, Nebraska and want to go to Disney World for spring break. It seems like simple task, but unless you look at a map, plot out the best way to get there, and read road signs, you could conceivably roam aimlessly for the rest of your life without hitting Disney World.

Unfortunately, this is how most people exist in relationships. They drive aimlessly. They don't know where they want to go or how to get there. Your task is to figure that out. The best way is to examine what you don't want. That will lead you to what you do want. Then, discuss a fair plan with your partner on how you can get to a destination in a way that is acceptable to you both. Once you figure that out, you're half way there.

Remove Your Masks

We all wear masks. A mask is anything that hides who you really are. They can be deceptive words, actions, deeds, or even facial expressions. When put together, they form an image to the outside world of "who you are." However, it is not who you really are. We create these masks out of fear. We think that if we project our true self, it will result in loss, or, ultimately, you won't get what you want.

For illustration's sake, here is an example of a mask. A couple has been married for five years and has two children. While they both love the kids, the wife takes on much more of the child care duties than the husband. As time goes on, the wife grows resentful towards him. However, instead of saying something and working it out in an amicable manner, she smiles and pretends like she's the "perfect mother." She is wearing the "perfect mother" mask. She doesn't feel like it, but she acts that way out of fear.

All masks are repression. We repress our true feelings so others will accept us. Even if you are smiling when you really don't want to smile, you are wearing a mask. That is what the wife in the above scenario was doing. If you are doing anything other than being direct and honest, you are wearing a mask.

Explore the masks you wear in your relationship, because you can't change what you don't recognize. Here are the primary reasons to explore this issue: **1|** to learn why you wear them (it will always be related to some sort of fear), **2|** to learn the price of wearing that mask (it usually results in stress on yourself or the relationship), and **3|** to see if the mask(s) is valid anymore (even if it isn't, people continue to wear it simply out of habit).

Habit vs. Love

We have a friend who says that he is with his wife today simply because that's where he was yesterday. In other words, he's not staying married out of love but out of habit.

Does this sound like you? Are you with your partner out of habit? If so, have you given up? Maybe you have. Or, maybe you've read this book and found some new creative ways to repair your relationship. If you think your relationship will be nothing more than a bad habit, maybe it's time to let go.

Staying in the relationship may seem easier, but it's not truthful. The superficial nature of the connection you have left is probably very much out of balance. When relationships become out of balance, the result is usually a feeling of emptiness. If you think your relationship can't be repaired, think about making a courageous move. Think about finding something better.

In order for the Universe to bring you a better relationship, you must first create a vacuum. You've probably heard the saying, "The Universe hates a vacuum." In other words, if something is empty, it will seek to fill it. Once you do end the relationship, you must clear your energy. If you hold on to old resentment or feelings of nostalgia, you will fill your vacuum. As a result, you will not be able to fully allow anyone else into your life. So, be at peace with the ending, send your partner light and love and say, "Go with God."

It is frightening to say good-bye to someone who has been such a big part of your life. However, trust that the Universe will open the right doors for you if you take that risk. There are many people who can provide you with the right balance that you need to be happy.

Stop Codependency

The term "codependency" is usually associated with a person who is dependent on someone with an addiction. We want to re-define it for you. For the purpose of this book, we will define it as an addiction to relationships and/or a person.

A codependent person will attach their identity to the relationship. We know a woman whose boyfriend cheated on her. Of course, she was upset and complaining about her plight. So, we said to her, "Why don't you just leave him?" She looked us square in the eye and said, "It's better than being alone." That is a perfect example of a codependent person. To be so fearful of being by yourself that you will put up with unacceptable behavior is not a healthy way to live.

Codependent people are not only insecure alone, they are insecure when they are in relationships because they fear they might end up alone. If that sounds like you, you are probably always on the lookout for anything about your partner that will reassure you—their words or behavior. Codependent people think that if their mate assures them of their devotion, they can be certain of their future.

However, as the old saying goes, "The only thing that is constant in life is change." If a codependent person needs to be assured of their partner's future presence, then they are just wasting their time. There are no guarantees. Heck, your mate could get hit by a bus tomorrow—anyone could. Putting all your focus on keeping your partner around is just futile.

Codependent behavior is rooted in fear. Any kind of fear-based emotion is of a low vibrational rate, which means that it can only attract more negative circumstances into your life. Try to focus on positive aspects of your relationship and don't fear being alone, because, if you do, that's probably exactly where you'll end up.

Intermittent Reinforcement

You and your partner may be withdrawing from each other. You may have become hypersensitive to the wrong words, a negative look, or a sarcastic comment that causes your blood to boil. At the same time, one or both of you may not be sure you want to let the other go. So, occasionally, one or the other is warm and loving but not for long. When the emotional fatigue and bitterness rises to the surface, the fighting or withdrawal begins all over again.

This on-again, off-again process known as "intermittent reinforcement" makes you both crazy.

If it is any consolation, this situation will not last indefinitely. Your relationship will either get better or worse, which allows what you desire to become clearer — to repair the union at any cost or to decide it is beyond repair.

To help you move past the frustration of intermittent reinforcement, you need to decide what you want. In other words, you need to ask yourself a lot of difficult questions and to be truthful with yourself in answering. Here are the kinds of questions to ask yourself:

- If you partner does not change, are you willing to remain in the relationship?
- How long are you willing to work at it? Five years? Four years? Three years? Two years? One year?
- Assuming you said one year, is it realistic to assume that your partner might change in one year? Have they ever changed?
- If the answer is no, your relationship is terminal in one year.

Ask yourself additional realistic questions about how far you are willing to go to make your relationship work. What must your partner be willing to do? What are you willing to do? Are you fantasizing about a new life without your partner? Are you attracted to someone new who is drawing upon your energy?

Role Play

Be Your Partner and Vice Versa

During relationship conflicts, a major problem is that each partner thinks they are "right." But, the real problem is that both people are "right." How can that be? Well, if you live by the motto that "perception is reality," everyone is always "right" because each one of us has our own unique perception of reality that is our own truth.

Obviously, this presents a problem. If you come to the realization that both of you are always "right," how does that work? The answer lies in developing empathy. Simply put, empathy is, "walking in another person's shoes." It's not enough to just say you understand the other person's point of view, you have to feel it.

The best way to do this is to role play. Let's take an example. A couple is having a fight because his daughter (her stepdaughter) has unexpectedly announced that she wants to move in with them in a few days. The wife is upset for two reasons: **1|** her husband merely "informed" her of the decision rather than talking to her about it first, and **2|** she has no time to prepare for this transition. The husband is upset because: **1|** he thinks she should just automatically accept his decision without questioning it because she know he misses his daughter and longs to be with her, and **2|** he thinks she is insensitive to his feelings and, ultimately, is being unreasonable.

Because there are such deep emotions connected to a situation like this, both people should sit down and "be the other person." He should explain the situation (to her) from her point of view, and she needs to do the same (to him). The purpose of this activity is to force each partner to actually slip into the mindset of the other. This exercise is highly effective as it leads to a greater understanding of the entire situation.

Happiness

"More than anything else, people seek happiness," says Mihaly Csikszentmihalyi in his book, *Flow*. The author spent 20 years researching topics related to the psychology of optimal experience.

Happiness is sought for its own sake, but all our other goals—health, beauty, money or power—are valued because we expect they will make us happy. Mihaly began his happiness research by studying hundreds of "experts"—artists, athletes, musicians, chess masters, and surgeons—in other words people who spend their time doing the activities they prefer. From their accounts, he developed a theory of optimal experience based on what he calls flow—"the state in which people are so involved in an activity that nothing else seems to matter; the experience itself is so enjoyable that people will do it even at great cost, for the sheer sake of doing it."

Further research indicated that flow wasn't limited to experts. Men and women, rich and poor, young and old, regardless of culture, can experience flow. The flow research included old women in Korea, adults in Thailand and India, teenagers in Tokyo, Navajo sheepherders, and people working on assembly lines in Chicago. The research concludes that the happiest people spend much time in a state of flow.

When psychic energy (attention) is invested in realistic goals and your skills match the opportunities for action, flow results. The pursuit of your goals brings such intense concentration that you momentarily forget everything else. Time disappears. In so doing, you achieve control over your psychic energy and, by stretching skills and reaching toward higher challenges, you become an increasingly extraordinary individual.

The flow research clearly states that people who regularly experience flow are stronger people who can more easily handle life's ups and down without caving in. To fully enjoy your life, learn to transform your activities into flow.

Happiness II

On the previous page we talked about the value of flow to generate more happiness in your life. Those who flow focus their attention intentionally upon the task at hand. It really amounts to knowing your goal, concentrating on it, remaining determined, and having the self-discipline to complete what you are doing.

You create yourself by how you invest your energy. When it is under control, your attention is focused. Attention is your most important tool in the task of improving the quality of your experience.

1. Choose a task that you have a good chance of completing.
2. You need the ability to focus your concentration upon the task at hand.
3. Clear goals are necessary, allowing you to focus your concentration.
4. The task provides feedback, which allows you to focus your concentration.
5. You get so involved in the task that you forget about everything else.
6. The task allows you to exercise a sense of control over your actions.
7. You become so focused on the task that self-concern disappears. (Your sense of self returns, stronger than ever after the flow experience is completed.)
8. You lose your sense of time; hours seem to pass in minutes, minutes can stretch out and seem like hours.

The combination of these factors causes a sense of deep enjoyment that is intensely gratifying. With this knowledge, it's possible to achieve control of consciousness and turn even routine tasks into an experience of flow.

Remember, flow is when all your relevant skills are needed to cope with the challenges of a task, and you become completely absorbed by the activity. No attention is left to process any information but what the activity offers.

Once you are flowing, the experience drives you on to more creativity and achievement. The development of increasingly refined skills to sustain enjoyment is the actual power behind the evolution of culture.

Youthful Energy

When people age, they begin to lose their youthful energy. Think about how you looked at the world when you were young; there were endless possibilities. It was exciting. The world was your oyster. Life was an adventure. Somewhere along the line, most people lose this outlook when they get older and enter into long-term relationships.

Joy, happiness, and harmony are youthful energies. Boredom, depression, and disharmony are aged ones. Your body may age, but that doesn't mean your spirit has to. A 75 year old man can be more youthful and alive than a 25 year old man if his attitude is positive and exciting.

When you are youthful, you are more adventurous, and as a result, you experience more aliveness. Young people typically take more risks. They feel immortal. It's that attitude that makes our lives worth living. If you allow yourself to become old in spirit (even if you are youthful in chronological age), you begin to let fear drift into your existence. You start to settle for security, comfort, and predictability instead of growth opportunities.

Not only does this happen to individuals, it happens to relationships too. In the beginning, the people are in love, they think they are invincible, and they feel as if they are walking on air. That is youthful energy. As the relationship progresses, they find themselves stagnating and sliding into boredom. That is old energy.

The key is to figure out how to bring this positive energy back. It starts with working on yourself first. You must be joyous and full of life before you can bring it into your relationship. The same is true for your partner. You must find people and activities that create this youthfulness. Once you do, you can become more positive about life, and this will spill over into your relationship as well.

Comfort and Discomfort

We all want to be perfectly comfortable in our relationships and, above all, we want to avoid discomfort in our unions. If we could, we would, but the outcome might not be all that desirable.

In his book *Actualizations*, Stewart Emery says, "Researchers have discovered that if you place an amoeba in an environment in which it is subjected to a great deal of discomfort, it will die. This is perhaps not at all surprising; the same is true of you and me. If you and I dwell in an environment that subjects us to constant discomfort, to pain, to constant put-downs and belittlement, our spirit for living will die. The surprise comes when we examine the results of placing an amoeba in an environment that provides it with absolute and continuous comfort. The result is the death of the amoeba. Again, there is a direct parallel with the results of a similar situation in human life. If you and I give in to an addiction for comfort, our spirit for life will die. If our spirit for living dies, we will find ways to arrange that our bodies also die."

Amoebas need to exist in a balanced environment of comfort and discomfort, just as humans do—especially humans desiring to achieve self-actualization.

Emery says, "What I observe as true for those people who are committed to a path of growth is that their experience of discomfort is exhilarating in a very healthy way. These people are excited about making the growth choice rather than constantly seeking the protection of the fear choice. These people find as they travel down the path that discomfort is sometimes a companion, though seldom for extensive periods. And on the other side of discomfort they discover a new high waiting for them, together with a deeper sense of their own self-worth."

If your relationship is not as comfortable as you would like it to be, it may be a blessing. Consider a new viewpoint.

Love vs. Scarcity

In a poor relationship, it is easy to focus energy on the scarcity of some element—love, affection, respect, etc. However, putting your attention toward lack will only perpetuate it. Instead, if you focus on love, you embrace your partner's value. If you think back on anything or anyone that you have loved, there is always a value there. If you loved your first car, it's because it meant something to you. If you love your best friend, it's because she/he contributes positively to your life. Whether it's a car, your best friend, a piece of pizza, or an ice cold beer, the reason you say you love it is because it is valuable to you.

While love begins with a recognition and appreciation of value, scarcity is a much different attitude. Instead, it is an intention to judge. For example, if you perceive a lack of affection from your partner, you are inherently judging him/her for that lack. You think, "If only he would hold my hand or cuddle with me more," and this is a focus on judgment. You are judging him for withholding his affection. When you judge, you have an "agenda" and a "fighting" approach to relationships. You will always feel the need to compete with or control your mate.

You should also look within and see how this applies to your personal love and value. Do you love yourself? If not, you probably attracted a partner who doesn't much either. Do you value yourself? If not, your partner probably doesn't value you either. These attitudes, whether it's toward yourself or toward your partner, are all connected at the very core.

Love sees value in everything, it attracts everything. Scarcity doesn't value anything, and it repels anything. Love embraces people and experiences. Scarcity keeps looking for something better. Think about how you approach your relationship—through love or scarcity.

Equality

In today's society, it is not politically correct to say that you don't want to be in an equal partnership. The days of the man being dominant and the woman being submissive are long gone. Or are they?

In our opinion, those days are not gone. People like to think they are. They even act that way in public just to keep up the illusion. When we interview married individuals, we have found that women, in particular, do not think there is equality in their relationship.

An attitude of equality comes from recognizing your own self worth while giving the same amount of worth to others. You must consciously acknowledge and appreciate that all people are valuable—including yourself. When we take on the attitude of equality, we tolerate, accept, and have compassion for others. This does not just mean in your thoughts but in your actions.

The word 'actions' was emphasized in the above paragraph because it is key to equality. You can sit and talk about how you think your partner is equal to you but to see whether or not it is really true, take a look at your actions. Do you share equal responsibility for everything in your joint life? Do you devalue or disrespect your partner in any way through your words or actions? If so, then you are not living equality. You think you are, but you are not.

Here is an easy way to see if you are living out equality—ask your partner. If he/she doesn't feel there is equality, then it doesn't matter what you think. A stamp of approval on how you treat your partner as an equal can only come from your partner -- not you.

Take some time to think about how you express—or don't express—equality in your relationship. Then take the steps to make it better.

Don't Argue With Feelings

Humans have two distinct sides: emotional and logical. They are two halves of a whole, but they often do not seem to fit together. We can have feelings that we don't understand. We may cry, yet our logical side is saying, "Hey, what the heck are you crying for? That doesn't make any sense."

Let's take a real life example. A couple we know has a recurring conflict. Karen has a "quirk," as she affectionately calls it. Her quirk is that she doesn't like to share her food. When she and her husband go to the movies, she always likes to get popcorn. Before they get there, she asks him if he wants to eat popcorn. His usual response is "no." So, Karen happily gets her own, and they sit down in the theater. A few minutes later, when Karen sees Barry's hand in her popcorn, she has feelings of anger. When she expresses herself to Barry, he gets mad at her because he thinks it's ridiculous that she won't share her food with him.

Karen has tried to explain to him that she knows her feelings are not logical. She acknowledges that there is no rational reason she should feel angry if her husband wants to share the popcorn, but her attitude is, "If he wanted popcorn, I would rather buy him his own instead of having him eat mine." His attitude is, "We're married. Married couples share things. Why can't she get over it and just give me a few measly kernels of popcorn without having a hissy fit?"

You can see here the difference between logic and emotion. Barry is arguing with emotion by trying to use logic. In a situation like this, you can't argue with emotion. Karen's emotion isn't based in logic. It simply is. There will be times when you have to remember this too. You can't argue with emotion.

Physical Conditions

That Cause Relationship Problems

A physical examination and blood tests can disclose conditions that are conducive to relationship problems. As an example, simple anemia, which is a reduction in either the number of red blood cells or the amount of hemoglobin in the blood, also generates a decrease in the amount of oxygen in the blood. As a result, your energy level drops, you can experience depression and a diminished sexual drive, among numerous other symptoms.

Check with your doctor about how to best treat this problem. Nutritionists usually have women increase their iron intake. Other suggestions include taking raw liver extract, which can be purchased at health food stores (500 mg twice daily). Others suggest supplements including, folic acid plus biotin, B12, Vitamin B complex, and Vitamin C.

Hypoglycemia (low blood sugar) is a common condition affecting more and more people because of their poor dietary habits, such as eating large quantities of simple carbohydrates: sugars, food made with white flour, caffeine, and soft drinks. High stress contributes to this condition.

People with hypoglycemia tend to be aggressive and lose their tempers easily, usually a few hours after eating sweets or fats, or drinking alcohol. Other symptoms include feeling shaky or almost desperately craving something to eat, especially sweets. Additional behavioral problems most likely to work against a relationship are irritability, fatigue, nervous habits, and metal disturbances.

To diagnose hypoglycemia, a doctor can perform a glucose tolerance test. The most common holistic approach to resolving the problem is to stop eating sugar in any form and commit to positive dietary change: eat smaller meals more often and increase your protein and vegetable intake. Suggested supplements include, brewer's yeast, chromium picolinate, pancreatin, proteolytic enzymes, vitamin B complex, zinc, vitamin E, calcium, and vitamin C.

There are dozens of other physical conditions that affect behavior and attitude. If this "repair" strikes a chord within you, consider a physical checkup for both you and your partner.

Accountability

We often blame the state of our relationship on our partner. We think, "It is their fault, not mine!" After all, if it wasn't their "fault," then we wouldn't be unhappy, right? Wrong.

Your relationship problems are just as much your fault as they are your partner's. Relationships are systems. Each component (person) affects the other component (person). Imagine if you cut a vital wire in a car, it probably wouldn't run anymore. Thus, the change in that one wire affected the entire car (system). The same is true for relationships. Each person's actions generate future actions from their partner.

Let's take an affair as an example. One partner had an affair, and it hurt the relationship. Most people in our culture automatically point the finger at the "dirty rotten scoundrel" who cheated on the poor innocent "victim." However, while the cheating partner certainly has the ability to control their actions, the "cheated-on" partner also has just as much responsibility for the cheating.

That statement probably infuriates most readers. However, if the relationship were in a satisfactory state to both partners, cheating would most likely not occur. Thus, while the "cheated-on" partner did not control the "cheater's" actions, he/she did contribute to the state of the relationship that led to the cheating.

Each person must open up the lines of communication and talk about the state of the relationship. Many people (especially men) do not like doing this. However, if you let it go, affairs are a likely outcome, not to mention other negative events.

To really drive home the need for accountability, let's make an analogy. Think of your relationship as a "third entity." There is you, your partner, and then there is "the relationship." Just as plants or children need attention and food to grow, so do relationships. The only difference is that both people must contribute equally to the nurturing of the relationship.

Increase Your Self-Discipline

Most people do not have much self-discipline. This is unfortunate because a successful relationship requires a great amount of it. We do not usually associate the word "self-discipline" with relationships, but rather with things such as dieting, exercising, or working the way up the corporate ladder.

When people get married, the vast majority sit back and subconsciously think, "Oh good! The work is over. I can just kick back, relax, and enjoy life and my relationship because the dating stage is over." That could not be farther from the truth. Marriage is not where the work stops. It is where the work begins.

People lack the self-discipline for putting effort into making the relationship work. In the beginning, it was fun to cook dinner for your lover or to bring them flowers. After a while, and especially after marriage, it becomes "work" for most. The lack of effort is reflected in one or both partners' attitudes and generally leads to a downward spiral if it is not caught and dealt with.

When someone interviews for a job, they put forth their "best." Once they are hired, they still need to perform. If they don't, they risk losing their job. For some reason, people do not feel the same pressure for "performing" at their relationships. Instead they take their partner and the relationship for granted. The mindset of "No Work Required Unless I'm Forced To" takes over.

You must find the self-discipline to work on your relationship. If you don't, you might as well face the fact that it is doomed, and it is just a matter of time before it ends. Are you willing to accept the ultimate demise of your relationship? If not, you better take a long hard look inside. Where is your self-discipline? You better go find it.

Control Your Subpersonalities

When someone says to you, "you have a great personality," it is a misleading statement. It implies that you have ***one*** "personality." You don't. No one does. We all have many. This does not mean that you are a schizophrenic with multiple split identities, but you do have sub-parts of yourself that could be sabotaging your relationship.

Let's take some common examples: the "critic," the "complainer," and the "control freak." Perhaps you have some, and maybe all, of these personalities. The critic comes out when your partner does anything that dissatisfies you. He left his stinky underwear in the middle of the floor again or has spent all day watching sports and hasn't said one word to you. Or, she is trying to tell you about her girlfriend's relationship problems while you are trying to watch the Super Bowl. We all have a critic that comes out quite often. Whether or not you share your thoughts with your partner, you are both still are experiencing the negativity.

The "complainer" is a subpersonality that likes to replay its problems over and over to anyone who will listen. This could be to your mate or even to your co-workers. The "complainer" is also negative. As long as you complain about something, you are not doing anything positive to repair the situation. You are just programming more negativity into your brain.

The "control freak" can emerge in many different ways. Some are overt, such as leaving a list of chores for your partner to do around the house while you are gone. Others are covert, such as withholding sex because he watches sports. Either way, trying to control someone else's actions never works. It generates resentment, which never helps any relationship.

Analyzing your subpersonalities will help you understand their nature and how to control them. By doing so, you will generate more positive feelings between you and your partner.

Create Aliveness

One of the things that most people lack in their lives, and certainly in their relationships, is aliveness. Aliveness is finding excitement and enjoyment in everything you do. It is that blood-pumping, exhilaration, challenge, joy, stimulation, and pleasure that makes life worth living. Most people don't feel aliveness. They feel boredom. If you ask some people how they are doing, you are likely to get a response similar to this: "Oh, I'm just going through the motions." What that is really saying is that the person is in a boring pattern. That is no kind of life.

You probably are "going through the motions" in your relationship. Most people are. They act like a machine; every day, they do the same thing. When two people, who are supposed to be in love, fall into this boring pattern, they must find a way to get out of it.

When a relationship is new, it is easy to find aliveness. It is natural and effortless. As the relationship continues, that newness wears off, and along with it, people's aliveness. But this doesn't have to happen. It only happens because you allow it to happen.

Humans have a strange tension between predictability and novelty. We like our lives to be predictable, but when it becomes too much so, we crave novelty. Unfortunately, many people ignore this craving in their relationships. They see it as too much work, or they just don't know how to respond.

Whether it seems like work to you or not, you must think about how you can create aliveness in your relationship. What works for one couple probably won't work for another. However, whatever you end up doing, it must be unexpected, new, different, and fun. If it feels good, do it. If it feels bad or neutral, stay away from it. Good, high, positive emotions tell you that you are creating aliveness.

Make the Right Choices

Life is filled with choices. At an intellectual level, everyone knows that. However, more often than not, people feel like victims who are at the mercy of others and outside circumstances. This seems to limit their options, but your life is made up of all the decisions you have ever made. The most important choices of all, at least in your relationships, are your behavioral choices.

If your partner does something, and you express anger towards him/her as a result, it is likely that you will say, "You really know how to get under my skin! Why do you make me so angry?" You probably even do a little yelling, screaming, or using of bad words to express the dissatisfaction that your partner "made" you angry.

Your partner did not make you angry. You allowed his or her actions to affect you and to culminate in the outward expression of anger. You made that choice. You could have responded with kind words and actions, or you could have responded with anger and blame. You chose, as do most people, the latter.

Allowing your partner to "push your buttons" like this takes away your power. By letting them send you "off kilter," you deny yourself a peaceful, balanced way of living. Is it really worth it? Wouldn't it be great to say, "I won't let you make me angry. I choose my emotions. I am choosing happiness and joy no matter what you do." Now that is power.

There are endless examples of the choices we make in relationships. You must claim your power and make sure you make a wise decision. Every action (or non-action) we take has an effect. So take time to think about the consequences of your choices. The ultimate goal is to be happy. Don't let a day go by without making the decision to keep yourself on that path.

Be Direct & Honest

One of the most difficult things to do in relationships is to be direct and honest for the following reasons:

- We don't want to hurt the other person's feelings.
- We want our partner to be a "mind reader" — to know what we want without having to tell them.
- We don't want to get ourselves "in trouble" by expressing our opinions.
- We might not even know what we want. If this is the case, we can express them directly.

According to gender research, the first two are more specific to women. This is because they are "relationship-oriented." The reason for this is both biological and cultural. Biologically, women are wired to take care of the young. So, paying attention to subtle emotional changes could have meant the difference between life and death in Cave-Man days. Culturally, this characteristic has been perpetuated in many societies over millions of years.

The last two statements are more specific to men. Generally, men are more "task-oriented" instead of "relationship-oriented." As a Cave-Man, the male had to be very task-oriented to concentrate upon killing the prey for dinner, and this has played out in modern society like this: When a man's wife comes home and wants to vent about what happened to her that day, he instinctually tries to offer her advice and fix her problems. That is "task-oriented."

Mind-reading is not something most humans are good at. Take ownership for your viewpoint and don't make your statements feel like criticism. If you want a Coke out of the refrigerator, ask. Don't succumb to the mind set of, "If he loved me enough, he would know I'm thirsty and automatically bring me a Coke." It doesn't work that way.

Be direct and honest in a way that empowers you both. Placing blame is not a positive way to express your feelings.

Be mindful of the way you would like to hear it and deliver it that way to your partner.

Judging Others

We know judgment is wrong, yet our experiences put us in the position of making judgments. When these are expressed verbally, we preface our statements with, "I'm not judging him, but..." as if that makes the judgment acceptable.

But the truth of the matter is, not all judgments are undesirable.

There are three kinds of judgments you do not want to make:

1. Judgments based upon your expectations.
2. Judgments that result in trying to change someone else.
3. Judgments generated by fear-based emotions.

These judgments echo your ideas of right and wrong and your desire to control. Rising above judgment doesn't mean you stop deciding what does and doesn't work for you. There are only so many hours in each day, and, if you're intelligent, you'll spend what time you have efficiently and pleasurably. If I said, "I don't want to spend time with John, because I no longer enjoy his company," you probably would not have a problem with the statement.

If I said, "John is a controller who dominates every conversation," you'd accuse me of being judgmental. But that's why I don't want to spend time with John. I'm not judging him to be wrong for dominating conversations and wanting to control situations, but I know it's wrong for me to spend time with him. I don't expect him to be anything other than what he is, and I have no desire to change him.

The metaphysical ideal is to accept other human beings as they are without judgments, expectations, blame, or attempting to control. With this understanding of judgment, the goal of unconditional acceptance is a little more realistic. Even John can qualify.

Four Ways Vanquish Anger

Take the time to notice that every time you got angry it is because you are not getting what you want.

You do not want to repress such a strong emotion as anger. Repressed emotions fester within and always end up surfacing in some undesirable way such as ulcers, depression, or misdirected antagonism. Long-term repression can cause cancer.

The idea is to learn to control anger so it doesn't destroy your relationships, raise your blood pressure, and come back to you in the form of cause and effect.

What can you do to deprogram anger? A good place to start is by reminding yourself when you get angry that your expectations are in conflict with what is. Maybe the other person is a jerk. That's what is. The other person is incompetent. That's what is. The other person is inconsiderate and selfish. That's what is. You can resist what is, blow your top and raise your blood pressure, but it won't change what is. In other words, your anger will probably only make matters worse.

Second, we suggest mind programming with self-hypnosis or directed meditation. Some people have greatly reduced their anger levels by chanting a mantra such as, "From now on, I choose to respond to negativity with tranquility." Say it over and over and over to yourself throughout the day—ideally, hundreds of times a day. Then, when you encounter an anger-inducing situation, the programming will click in.

Running is a Tibetan cure for anger. If you're in an office, rush up and down the stairs. If you're at home, run around the house or around the block. Exertion requires more oxygen. When your breathing changes, your thought patterns change. If you can't run, do some deep breathing.

The idea is to learn to control your anger or it will control you.

Stress

Beliefs are the basis of reality. They generate thoughts and emotions, which in turn create all your experiences. It is that simple; there are no exceptions. Your beliefs are the result of programming from your current incarnation and from your past lives. Many of your beliefs are faulty and self-defeating. They are blocks to your happiness and success. If you're not satisfied with your life, you need to begin the process of reinvention by changing beliefs.

Stress manifests as a conflict between beliefs: **1|** We have a belief about how things are, and **2|** we have a belief about how things *should* be. When these two beliefs do not align, the result is stress.

Your belief about how something is, is not necessarily reality. You may think it is reality, but that doesn't make it so. Reality just is. You cannot change what is. If there is no possibility of changing it, why resist it? Remember Buddha's words: "It is your resistance to what is that causes your suffering."

Stress is caused by a conflict between your interpretation of reality and your expectations of how things should be.

EXERCISE **1|** Recall a recent stressful experience. **2|** Capture the emotions that accompanied the experience. **3|** Explore your belief about how things were (your perception of reality). **4|** Explore your belief about how the situation or the other person should have been. **5|** Explore the conflict between the two that caused the stress. **6|** Consider the experience from the perspective of your expectations being in conflict with what is (reality).

Look in the "Mirror"

Other people are a mirror for you to see yourself. The traits you respond to in others are ones you recognize in yourself. When you look at your mate, you see yourself—for better or for worse.

The mirror has two manifestations: **1**| Characteristics you admire in others exist within yourself, and **2**| That which you resist in others is sure to be found within yourself. Let's take an example. Eva is married to Robert. She admires his fun-loving attitude and sense of humor. Those are the qualities that attracted her to him from the start. However, she feels Robert also has a tendency to be lazy, selfish, and unmotivated. These latter qualities cause them problems. She feels he will do nothing around the house or with the kids unless he is forced to (lazy and unmotivated). He seems to always be concerned with his own desires rather than hers. If he is at a family gathering, he will expect her to take care of the kids the entire day and night while he parties with his brothers (selfish).

If Eva took a close look at herself, she would probably find that she is afraid these qualities also exist within her. While she keeps a clean house, she hates every minute of it and would probably let her husband do it all if he didn't resist (she's afraid she's just as lazy). She certainly knows that if she had an opportunity to party with her sisters (without negative repercussions from Robert), she would take advantage of it.

In conclusion, even though on the surface Eva seems much "better" than Robert in the lazy and selfishness departments, she secretly fears that she is just as bad as he is. As a result of looking in the mirror (at Robert), anger is manifested in the relationship.

What lessons can be learned by seeing yourself in your partner?

Don't Try to Change Your Partner

In relationships, people often think along these lines, "If only Tom was more affectionate, we would be happily married" or "If Steve would just stay home with me instead of playing golf all the time, I would be happier." Notice the "if only my partner were different" part of those sentences. That is where you get into trouble.

Here is a newsflash: Your partner is acceptable as is. It is you who has the problem. In order for you to accept that statement, let's turn it around. Would you say that there are things about you that your partner would like to change? Do you think he/she thinks you're perfect? It is unlikely that any mate thinks their counterpart is perfect. It is safe to conclude that your partner would probably like to change a few things about you, too.

Do you think you are acceptable as you are? Most people would probably answer "yes" to that statement. If you think you are acceptable, don't you think your partner thinks they are acceptable too? There lies the paradox: you are both acceptable as you are. You are acceptable. Your partner is acceptable. Why do you resist?

A philosophy to live by that has been echoed throughout this book is: It is your resistance to what is that causes your suffering. You are resisting how your partner is, and that is causing the suffering in your relationship.

You cannot change other people; they only change if they want to. What you can change is your viewpoint. Adopt the attitude of, "It's okay for my partner to be the way he is. It's alright for me to not be affected by his actions." By changing your viewpoint, you can transform the way you see your relationship. If you're no longer affected by the "problem," then you no longer have a problem.

Don't Take Things Personally

When a woman wants to talk about "the state of the relationship" with her partner, he usually freezes up and thinks, "Oh God. What did I do wrong now?" He probably clams up and is ready to be on the defensive. This demonstrates how we automatically assume that our partner is criticizing us. You must keep in mind, however, that talking about the state of the relationship does not necessarily mean you did something wrong.

The only way this viewpoint works is if both people adopt this attitude. If one partner is talking about the "state of the relationship," it is easy to blame the other for the problems. There are no innocent victims; both of you are responsible for the state of the relationship.

If you are the one beginning a conversation about something, be sure you always use "I language." "I-language" is taking responsibility for your feelings. Instead of saying, "I can't believe you didn't call me to tell me you were coming home late from work," say "When you didn't call me to say you were going to be late, I got worried. I felt scared that something happened to you." Notice how the two are very different. The first statement is accusatory. The last statement is focusing on yourself instead of the other person's character.

If for some reason your partner doesn't use "I-language," simply refuse to take what they say personally. In the above example, perhaps that person would be mad at anyone who did not call when they were going to be late. Therefore, it is not you, but rather your actions (and what they represent to the other person) that bothers them.

Take the focus off yourself and put it on the relationship. Work as a team. Be respectful when you deliver information. De-personalize it. If your partner tries to place blame on you, simply refuse to buy into it.

Be an Inspiration to Your Partner

If your partner does not satisfy your expectations, stop and think: are you living up to your own expectations? It is so easy to point your finger at the other person and say "It's all your fault." But, remember that this is a partnership. You are a team.

One way to generate a more positive atmosphere is to inspire. If you are upset by "unacceptable" behaviors in your partner, you must first model them yourself. You can encourage your partner to cooperate and become more than they think they can be.

For example, perhaps you think your partner does not pay enough attention to you. He frequently goes golfing, watches sports, or socializes with his friends. All you do is moan and groan and complain, both to him and to your friends. How much attention are you paying to him? Have you tried to become what you want him to be?

Take a look at the things you do. What do you do when he is otherwise occupied? Are you sitting at home twiddling your thumbs, or are you doing something else too? Maybe you use his absence as an opportunity to "escape." In fact, your partner could be saying the same thing about you behind your back. Perhaps, he thinks you don't make enough time to spend with him.

It could be a vicious circle. You don't make time to spend with him because he doesn't make time to spend with you. Maybe he doesn't make time to spend with you because you don't make time to spend with him. You may both be mirroring the other person's actions without realizing it.

Who "started" these actions first doesn't really matter. The only thing that does is the fact that you need to change your behavior. If you do that, the other person will follow suit.

Become More Empathic

Empathy is not the same thing as sympathy. Sympathy is when you feel sorry for someone. For example, if a family member dies, you send them a sympathy card saying "I'm sorry." That is not empathy. You can feel badly for someone without being able to identify with their experience — that's the difference between sympathy and empathy. Empathy is the ability to "put yourself in the other person's shoes." Most people are not very empathic, especially in romantic relationships. This is one of the major problems you need to overcome.

According to research, the majority of us think that women are more empathic than men. This is not true. However, that does not mean that men are more empathic than women. The most empathic people are androgynous — meaning, they have equal sets of both masculine and feminine behaviors, regardless of their sex. These people can identify with more types of behaviors than the people who lie at the very feminine or very masculine end. They have a better understanding of both, so they are able to relate to other people more effectively.

Even if you're not a very androgynous person, you can learn to be more empathic. All you need to do is become aware of when you are only looking at things from your perspective. Remember how important it is to you that your partner see the situation from your point of view and give them the same courtesy.

We can't emphasize enough how important empathy is to a good relationship. If you can't identify with the other person (or at least pretend to), they won't feel "heard." They will feel defensive, and the relationship will be damaged as a result. You have to live by the motto that "perception is reality." Your partner's perception is their reality just as much as your perception is yours. Empathy is key to having a happy and successful relationship.

What You Deny to Your Partner Will be Denied to You

You could probably make a long list of things that are not going right in your relationship. They probably include things like: lack of affection, lack of respect, lack of sexual intimacy, lack of emotional intimacy, or lack of attention. Perhaps, it is all of the above, but the one common denominator of all of these problems include the word "lack."

It is likely that you feel that you are being denied your needs and desires, and you probably are. Maybe your husband never says he loves you or never does nice things for you (lack of affection and lack of emotional intimacy). Perhaps, your wife never wants to have sex with you and always talks to you as if you were an idiot (lack of sexual intimacy and lack of respect).

It is easy to sit and analyze how you are being denied in the relationship. However, what you should do is think about what you are denying your partner. Let's take the sexual example. Your wife (or husband) doesn't want to have sex with you anymore. You feel rejected, neglected, and unattractive. As a defense mechanism, you decide to act uninterested in sex as well. This may not have occurred on a conscious level, but, nonetheless, it has manifested through your actions. In essence, you are denying your mate of sexual intimacy just as much as he/se is to you.

If you feel you are being denied something in the relationship, instead of playing the victim role, turn the tables and take a look at yourself. You are probably responsible (at least partially) for what you are being denied. If you want to receive, you first have to know how to give it. Until you can understand that you will not get what you won't give, then you will be faced with a sub-par relationship.

Totally Commit

You have to make some serious decisions about your commitment to the relationship. Whether or not you are legally married, you have committed to your partner at some level. It may not have been spoken in front of a preacher and 300 guests in a church, but the unspoken agreement still exists.

Many people claim to be in committed relationships, but the level of dedication that is needed to really make relationships thrive usually does not exist. Partners think that just because "the ink is dry" on the marriage certificate or that they haven't officially broken up, that they are committed. That couldn't be farther from the truth.

You can be physically "committed" but emotionally "gone." This is often called an "emotional divorce." You are still living with, married to, or simply not officially broken up with your partner, but your feelings have gone a different direction. You are there in body but not in spirit.

This "emotional divorce" signals indecisiveness. You are not sure what you want out of this relationship anymore. You don't want to leave yet, otherwise you would have, but you aren't happy staying. So, the turmoil continues.

You have to make a decision—either totally commit to saving the relationship or let go. The "in-between" state that you are in is damaging to you both. If you partially commit, you can only experience partial joy. You should stop living with one foot in safety. If you're going to stay with your partner, stay and be there both physically and emotionally. If you're going to leave, then leave and make a decision and fully commit to it with no exceptions.

If you can't find a level of total dedication to your relationship, you might as well count on the fact that you will never have what you want. The relationship will either end, or it will continue to die a slow death.

Control Yourself

If you step back and look at your relationship from an intellectual standpoint, you know the right thing to do at each moment. You know that yelling, screaming, name-calling, avoidance, or withdrawal does not make for a happy relationship. You know that intellectually. The real challenge comes in convincing your emotional side that this is the best strategy to live by.

The problem lies in the fact that our emotions want us to feel good right now. Immediate gratification is an issue for most people. For example, if we say we are going to lose weight, we may start off well. We eat right and exercise. However, when you see that ice cream stand, your emotions scream out for you to eat a gooey hot fudge sundae. You give in, drive up to the restaurant, consume 1,500 calories, and blow your diet. This is immediate gratification.

Another example of immediate gratification is when someone has an affair. They meet someone who turns them on sexually. The other person even makes them feel interesting, attractive, and important. As a result, the emotional side of the person falls into the "affair trap." It feels good to have sex with them. It feels good to have their ego stroked by being wanted by someone other than their partner. This is immediate gratification.

We all succumb to immediate gratification in one way or another, even if it "feels good" at the moment to yell at our partner during a fight. When you let your emotional desire for immediate gratification control you, relationships don't work. The only way to take control is to understand how it works against you and make agreements with yourself and have the integrity to keep them. You either get results in your relationship or you create excuses to explain why it's not working. Which would you rather have: a life of excuses or a life of results?

Strive for Unconditional Love

Our goal is to learn to express unconditional love, because love is the highest emotion of all. The problem is that most of us don't even know how to define unconditional love, let alone live it.

Here are some characteristics of unconditional love:

- Your love for another person cannot be diminished by anything the other person said or did.
- Your love is not dependent upon being loved.
- Your give freely of yourself with no expectation of return.
- You allow total freedom to your mate.
- You expect no more than your lover can give.
- You love your partner without expecting him/her to change.
- You find joy in your partner's happiness, even at the expense of your own.
- You rise above any and all negativity, refusing to let it affect you.

How many of these can you honestly say you do? Probably not many. Let's take a look at an extreme example to help bring unconditional love to life. Your partner had an affair. Instead of "making him pay" for his actions, you accept the fact that he had needs that were unfulfilled. You know that the both of you had equal responsibility for making the relationship the way it is. You may decide to stay or decide to leave. If you decide to stay, you put the past behind you and move forward without "punishing" your mate. If you decide to leave, you let go with light and love. You wish your partner well and move on with your life without holding any resentment or hostility.

Unconditional love does not require you to stay in a bad relationship without having your needs fulfilled. Instead, it allows you to be light and free from negativity. You realize the other person is just doing their best, and you love them anyway. You have the right to stay or to leave.

Do Little Things

Often couples silently "keep score" of the things that go on in the relationship. For example, a husband may "score points" if he cleans the kitchen without being asked to do so. A wife may "score points" if she is easy-going about her husband going to play poker with his friends on Friday night.

We could advise you to not keep score. It is definitely the best thing to do — it would mean you were capable of unconditional love. Since that is not true of most of us, the next best thing we suggest is to make sure you do things for your partner not simply to "score" points, but because you love him/her.

The problem with "keeping score" is that both partners interpret certain actions differently. Giving the kids a bath at night may feel like a lot of points to a husband who does it, but, perhaps, the wife feels like that is something he should be doing as an equal partner anyway, so she doesn't give him nearly as much credit as he would like.

When we think in terms of score keeping, we usually look for the "big" things. Don't forget the little things. Yes, buying a new Ford Explorer for your wife for Valentine's Day is very nice. Perhaps, she would be just as happy if you brought her home a rose from work one day.

Any little thing you can do for your partner that you know your partner would like is the most important thing you can do. It shows you pay attention to the very core of their being and know what is meaningful to them.

Chances are that neither of you go out of your way to do a small act of love for no other reason than to make your partner happy. But remember, a little act of love can go a long way.

Live for Your Partner, Not Yourself

Just because you are still with your partner does not mean that either of you are living for the other person. Even though you are "here," one or both of you are mentally "gone." If this sounds like your relationship, try to analyze when you got lost. What happened? There may have been an "event" or a series of events that led to the mental state of both of you. If this is true, try to think of things you can do about it now, if anything can be done.

Perhaps, one of the main reasons one or both of you are "mentally gone" from the relationship is because you had different expectations of what marriage was going to be. You thought you married one person, yet he/she turned out to be someone completely different. If this is true, you need to figure out who is the "true" person: the first or the second. If it is the latter, you have to realize that your partner may never change. This does not mean that you shouldn't try to repair the relationship, but it does mean that you might need to consider other options if it doesn't work.

It might be you who is "mentally gone." If so, you are probably living for yourself and not your partner. Maybe your mate seems distant, depressed, or moody. If you notice these things, talk about it. It may be a silent cry for help—a plea to pay attention to him/her and the relationship.

Relationships are about so much more than merely occupying the same space. If you think you are blind to your partner's needs and desires, wake up. Wake up and work on the relationship. Wake up and acknowledge your selfishness. If you don't, you may hear your partner say goodbye because "all you live for is yourself, not me."

Detached Mind

There is *attached* mind and *detached* mind. Most people live out their lives knowing only attached mind. This means your state of mind is always changing from positive to negative as outside conditions change. You are fine one minute, but when your mate yells at you, you become sad. This is extreme fluctuation from happiness and joy down through neutral to the basement of emotions—anger, hostility, depression, et cetera.

The goal is to develop detached mind. This means your state of mind fluctuates only from positive to neutral as outside conditions change. You accept all the warmth and joy that life has to offer while detaching from negativity and allowing it to flow through you without affecting you. In other words, your state of mind drops no further than neutral.

Once you develop detached mind, you detach only from the negativity in your life. This does not mean that you do not experience feelings. We are not talking about repressing your natural negative emotions. As long as you feel anger, hostility, and resentment, you will have to express it, or it will turn inward and have to come out in another way.

Maybe your partner criticizes you. Normally, your emotions would sink, and you might respond in anger. If you come to realize that when you resist what is, you make matters worse. Instead of resisting, skip the drama and know that your partner's comments say a lot more about him than they do about you. You back off out of wisdom, not repression. By eliminating negativity, you leave more room for love and warm interaction, and you will be more likely to enter into what you do in life with nothing held back—free to be entirely at one with your circumstances.

To develop detached mind, accept total responsibility for what you experience, learn to accept what is and know that the way you view life will result in how you experience life—either positively or negatively.

Consider Your Ego

"The stronger your ego, the more problems in your life," says Lama Zopa Rinpoche.

We define expressions of ego as expressions of fear-based emotions. Think about it. Your every egoistic thought, word, or action is generated by a fear-based emotion. How could it be otherwise?

Your mate says something that irritates you, and you respond curtly out of insecurity (a fear-based emotion). You fear your mate does not respect you enough, or your mate thinks he knows better than you, or what he said is true, or, maybe, the insecurity has generated an attachment that resulted in anger when your mate didn't live up to your expectations.

Maybe your mate is late, and you want to know why. Your ego demands your mate answer to you. Are you being possessive or jealous (both are fear-based emotions)?

If you work to rise above your fears, you rise above ego. This wisdom erases karma, and the more patient and compassionate you are, the easier it is to evolve beyond ego, which results in fewer problems in this life and future lives.

In his book *Virtue and Reality*, Rinpoche says, "By practicing Dharma today we also create the causes for our own happiness the happiness of this life, future lives, liberation and enlightenment. This is something we can do right now. Therefore, it is essential to create as much good karma as possible, while we have the chance. We should take every opportunity to create even the tiniest merit. Since we want even the smallest comfort, we have to create its cause. Similarly, since we don't want to experience even the smallest suffering or inconvenience, we have to avoid creating even the tiniest non-virtue."

Anger As Manipulation

Anger is an effective manipulation ploy when used against anyone unnerved by openly aggressive behavior. Your challenge when confronted with anger is to remain calm and respond assertively in an even voice.

"The psychological energy of anger comes from the real or imagined sense of threat," says David Richo in his book *How To Be An Adult*, "Anger is expressed actively when we show it directly. Usually this involves the raising of one's voice, changes in facial expression and gestures, and a show of excitement and displeasure. Anger can also be expressed passively, i.e. passive aggressively. One punishes the other without admitting one's anger, e.g. tardiness, gossip, silence, refusal to cooperate, absence, rejection, malice to cause pain, etc. Passive anger is inappropriate and not an adult way of behaving. Strongly expressed anger is called rage. Strongly held anger is called hate. Unexpressed anger is resentment. Anger can be unconsciously repressed and internalized. It then becomes depression, i.e. anger turned inward."

What kind of anger is your partner projecting at you?

What does their anger bring up in you?

As an example, if your partner becomes angry over the way you handled money, your self-esteem may be threatened. Maybe you fear their disapproval will ripple out into other aspects of your life and threaten your relationship. Maybe you fear physical abuse. Project all of your reactions so you can better understand what exactly you fear from their anger.

The only reason someone gets angry is because they want approval or they want to control your actions or reactions. This is not their right. View their anger as a manipulative ploy to control your behavior. Do not fall for it. Respond to anger with the Assertiveness Training Techniques in the back of this book.

Relationships As A Busy Street

In looking at your life, do you feel as if you're standing in the middle of a busy street, and noisy traffic is careening all around you? You're so busy avoiding the chaos that you don't take the time to understand your entrapment.

If you make your way out of the traffic by stepping up on the curb, you can observe all the movement and see that no matter how busy the street is, there are clear areas — breaks in the traffic. Next, imagine yourself going up to the fourth floor of a tall building and looking down upon the street. It looks different from here. There is direction and flow. From this perspective, it does not have much to do with you; it is just going on.

If you go up to the building and look down you see that the traffic is simply patterns. Other streets are also part of the patterns. Areas of difficulty, where the traffic gets stuck, are just part of the whole — not good nor bad, just part of life.

The more self-actualized you become, the more you can appreciate the flow, jam-ups, and patterns as what is. You learn to become a witness of life without getting caught up in the drama. From this perspective, you can see the confusion for what it is and return to the street in the middle of the traffic without being affected by it.

In *Everyday Zen*, Charlotte Joko Beck draws an analogy between the busy street and our relationships. We feel caught right in the middle of the traffic and confusion. Our relationships bring puzzlement and bitterness, because we expect them to be the one place that gives us peace from the traffic and chaos. Relationships are our best way to grow, because they can show us where we are stuck and what we are holding on to. Think of your relationship as a mirror of your life.

Respect & Reciprocity

When you are really committed to your relationship, you realize that what is necessary to your individual well being is also necessary for the health of the relationship. Successful relationships consist of rational and responsible people who know that in order for their connection to work, they must put forth effort while making their partner (and the relationship) a priority. Many partnerships are repairable if both people are willing to put in their 100% (notice we didn't say 50% — each has to put in 100% effort).

Two things are fundamental to any mutually nurturing relationship: respect and reciprocity. Without these, the possibility of a fulfilling relationship is very slim. This statement may seem simple and obvious, but, unfortunately, most relationships lack both of them.

Ask yourself some questions. Do you respect your partner? Does your partner respect you? If you had to think about either of those questions even for a split second, you have a problem. The reason it is so vital to assess respect is because if it doesn't exist, it is unlikely that the people will be willing to do the work it takes to improve the relationship. If you had to think about the level of respect, invest time to detect signs of disrespect and address them. Believe it or not, most people don't even notice.

Reciprocity is needed in any relationship. This can be in any area: love, sex, respect, household chores, child care duties, etc. If there isn't reciprocity, the relationship is out of balance, which means that one of you doesn't consider the other to be an equal partner. Somewhere in their subconscious, they must think they are superior.

Take some time to assess the level of respect and reciprocity in your relationship and decide to do something about it.

Sex is a Mirror

Does your sex life lack something? Are you at a loss for why? If you want answers, look outside the bedroom doors. The answer lies in the rest of your relationship.

Sex always mirrors other issues in your relationship. As Dr. Phil McGraw (aka "Dr. Phil") says, if you have a fulfilling relationship, sex becomes about 10% of the relationship (meaning there is no need to focus on its importance because it is flowing nicely). If you don't have a good relationship, sex becomes about 90% of the focus. If your sexual relationship isn't working, you better start looking at the other areas of your relationship that are suffering.

Your sex life isn't separable from the rest of the relationship. It is an integral part. In fact, it is almost impossible to have a happy, successful romantic relationship without a healthy sex life. You may think you can compartmentalize these aspects of your relationship, but it can only be done for so long. Lack of sexual intimacy will only create distance, and the longer it goes on, the farther the distance between the partners. There are married people who haven't had sex for 20 years. So, what's the point of being married?

Sexual problems aren't limited to the lack of sex either. Lack of quality sex is a problem. We hear many women complain that their husband wants to have sex, but it feels like he might as well have just used his hand. In other words, there was no intimacy or love created by the act. Unfortunately, many couples suffer from this phenomenon. If this is a problem in your relationship, one or both of you must become less selfish. Sure, it's great to feel good, but don't forget that there are two people involved. Both must have a positive experience, or else it's destructive to the relationship.

Make Making Love Special

When we first come together with a partner, we are usually overwhelmed with physical attraction. As time marches on, those feelings tend to fade. Perhaps, sex becomes routine at best and non-existent at worst. This familiarity can breed disinterest or even contempt.

As with any aspect of your relationship, you need to stay focused on making quality sex a priority. This means that you both realize that sex isn't limited to intercourse. Someone once said, "The brain is the most important sex organ." In other words, a sexual relationship isn't just about the sexual act. It's also about the psychological issues that surround the relationship.

There is a stereotype that men just want their wives to have sex and then fall asleep, and they don't understand why their wives don't want to make love at the end of the day. If you were to ask a woman why that is, she would probably say something to the effect of, "He ignores me all day, doesn't help with the kids, or do anything to make me happy, so why should I want to have sex with him?"

Consider changing your attitude about sex. Being in a loving relationship means making love in many ways. It doesn't even have to be sexual. Remember the days before you actually had sex? For most people, it was thrilling if someone held their hand or caressed them lightly. As we get older, most people just skip the fun, exciting stuff that was so great when we were young. Instead, they just jump into bed and start "going at it" without any tenderness leading up to it.

If your sex life is suffering, think about what you can do to create romance and excitement. Do little things. Say "thank you" and "I love you." Touch. Caress. Kiss. Pretend you're a kid again and have a make-out session with all your clothes on.

Be Present

You can't make a relationship work unless you are psychologically present. That means that you are "there" not just physically but emotionally. You need to be available to your partner not just for simple companionship but for intellectual stimulation, affection, and love. This is a huge problem for most couples, and the tricky part is that those who are not present are the last to admit it.

Our culture is very fast-paced. It is common to have both spouses working, even when they have children. As a result, they may not even see very much of each other. Because of this it, is very easy to become "unplugged" from the relationship. People rationalize the disconnect from their partner on their busy lives. They blame their problems on outside circumstances and not on their behavior.

You simply cannot have a quality relationship if you are never together. Even if you are physically together, if you're not emotionally connected, you are not present. If this goes on too long in a relationship, you will eventually look at your partner and see a stranger. You will look back and wonder how you got to that point. It is not uncommon for a couple to get divorced after all the kids have left the house. They have grown apart through the years, because they weren't present. It may have happened without their conscious knowledge.

If you don't want this happening to you, you better prioritize each other and the relationship. It takes planning and focus, but it can be done. If you don't make special quality time to be with your partner, you are simply saying that everything else in your life is more important. Is that the message you want to send?

Perception is Reality

When we are in conflict with our mate, we usually think they are wrong and we are right. In fact, most people will fight to the death to prove that their view is superior to their mate's. This behavior is probably one of the top three worst things you can do in a relationship.

In order to have a peaceful partnership, you must remember one vital thing: perception is reality. Let's look at an analogy to illustrate that objective reality does not exist. There is a tree in your yard. While no one may argue that there is a tree there (objective reality), everyone will come up with their own personal interpretation of it (subjective reality). In discussing the tree, one person may talk about how beautiful the leaves are and how tall the tree is. Another person will talk about the type of tree and how old it is. They are both talking about the same tree, but they are focusing on different aspects of the same reality. Neither of them is wrong. They are both right. Correct?

If we apply this analogy to relationships, why do we make our mate 'wrong'? They are just seeing the tree (relationship) from a different perspective. Correct? If you agree with this statement, you should not "fight to the death" to prove your point. Instead, simply acknowledge that it is your partner's right to interpret reality his/her own way. The same goes for you.

You do not have to agree with your partner, but you do have to acknowledge and affirm that their feelings are valid. You must accept that it is their truth. You don't want your truth to be denied to you, right? Why would you take that away from your partner?

Stop! Rate the Vibrations

When you encounter anger from your partner, you have a choice of mirroring their emotions, or you can remain centered and detached. Choose to acknowledge your partner's need to express and refuse to internalize their anger.

When you carry negative emotions, it affects the way you interact with everyone in your life. Internalizing anger generates stress, and, all too often, it becomes an emotional habit that can have an unhealthy impact on your body.

The next time you encounter anger do not instantly react. Instead, STOP! Take a deep breath and tune into the tone and level of the vibrations you find yourself experiencing. You might even want to rate the level of the vibrations on a scale of one to ten, with ten being the most positive. In such an environment you would feel relaxed, at ease and energized. If you rate the vibrations as a one, you are going to experience insecurity, lack of energy and cloudy thinking.

Trust how you rate the vibrations in any interpersonal encounter and try to keep them above a seven. In a lower vibration, refuse to be reactive and defensive. In the moment you take to stop and rate the vibrations, choose to be an adult and "in the moment." In so doing, maybe you can increase the level of vibration by being positive.

To carry this idea from your relationship to the outer world, check out the vibrational level of any situation or environment you find yourself in. It could be a group of people, a restaurant, or a purchase you plan to make. Rate it. If you are buying a book or renting a video, hold the object in your hand, take a deep breath, quiet your mind, and trust the vibrational number that comes in. If it is a higher number, you will enjoy it, or learn from it.

Take Psychological Responsibility

Research has shown that even in this "progressive" day, women still have more responsibility when it comes to taking care of the house/family. The amount of housework and childcare that husbands do has only risen from 20% to 30% over the last 30 years*. The only difference is, in the 1970s, many women weren't working outside the home. Back then, it made more sense for the man to "bring home the bacon" and for the woman to take care of the household and children.

Today, many women work outside the home. So, for the men to be helping them out so little with every day chores is taking a toll on the wives. While this is disturbing, there is an even more taxing burden that women tend to carry: psychological responsibility.

This term was coined by a study done in 1989.* Psychological responsibility is the task to remember, plan, and make sure things get done. For example, even though both partners may cook the family meals, the woman is mainly the one who has to plan the meals and shop for the food. Another example is that women are generally more responsible for remembering the children's doctor's appointments, soccer practice, and social calendars. This planning and organization is a psychological responsibility not usually accounted for in a couple's agreement for sharing the work of a family.

The consequences of this psychological responsibility are substantial. Women who take on more tasks than the men are more fatigued, stressed, and susceptible to illness. In addition, it affects the quality of the relationship. Resentment and conflict emerge when one partner is pulling more weight than the other.

Other research indicates that this type of inequality is a primary source of relationship dissatisfaction and instability. Take a moment to explore the responsibility each one of your carries and how that affects the overall quality of your relationship.

---

*Morin, R. & Rosenfeld, M. (1998, April 19). *Men and women: What still divides us?* Raleigh News and Observer. pp. 23A, 24A.

*Hochschild, A. (1989). *The economy of gratitude.* In D. Franks & E.D. McCarthy (Eds.), The sociology of emotions: Original essays and research papers (pp.95- 113). Greenwich, CT: JAI Press.

Autonomy vs. Connection

There has been much research conducted on basic human needs. One of the needs couples struggle with is in the tension between wanting autonomy from our partner and, at the same time, desiring connection. Leslie Baxter (1990), a gender scholar, has termed this phenomenon "dialectical tensions."

Both autonomy and connection are basic human needs. This in itself is problematic. However, it gets even more complicated when two people in a relationship have differing preferences for how much of each they will have. Males tend to want more autonomy and less connection than females. Females' needs tend to be the reverse. This is not to say that men only want autonomy, but they tend to want more of it than their partners. Both sexes want both, but the proportions vary.

The desire for different levels of autonomy and connection can generate friction in relationships. In fact, it is a common problem. This is the usual scenario: when one partner seeks emotional closeness through self disclosure and intimate communication, the other partner tends to feel suffocated. The result is a vicious cycle. The more closeness one demands, the more the other runs away. The more that person runs away, the more the other partner demands closeness.

Men are socialized to want and/or need independence. Women are socialized to pay attention to relationships. When a man pulls away, the woman will probably feel rejected. This is because each partner interprets the other's actions through their own lens of reality. The man might think, "If only she loved me, she would realize I need my space and leave me alone." The woman might think, "If only he loved me he would talk to me and be more intimate with me." This is where couples get into trouble.

Sit down with your mate and discuss how the two of you might be able to reach a compromise.

Baxter, L. (1990). Dialectical contradictions in relationship development. Journal of Social and Personal Relationships, 7, 143-158.

Women as "Relationship Experts"

In our culture, women are silently considered the "relationship experts." Just like many people assume all women are naturally maternal, they think they are naturally good at maintaining relationships. Research has indicated that this "unspoken" expectation has long been recognized in heterosexual relationships*.

Because women are expected to assume the role of "relationship expert," there is a burden placed on them. Research has confirmed that women assume the responsibility for maintaining relationships. They devote greater effort to keeping their partnership healthy. The stage of the relationship where men put in the most effort is in the beginning/dating phase. After that, both sexes assume that it is the female's responsibility.

Further evidence of this phenomenon comes from studies that are conducted on homosexual couples. Lesbian partners tend to assume mutual responsibility for nurturing the relationship and providing emotional support to their partners. This is because, like most heterosexual women, our culture has socialized lesbians to be sensitive to the dynamics of communication. Therefore, the level of satisfaction with relationships is higher among lesbians than among either heterosexual or gay (male-male) couples.

Like straight men, gay men are less adept at reading nuances of person-to-person interaction. Therefore, all men, regardless of sexual orientation, are less likely to monitor or nurture their relationship.

It's been argued that a major predictor of divorce wasn't how the husband felt about the intimate relationship, but how the wife felt, including how well she was able to communicate and self-disclose her inner self to her partner.

What does this mean for your relationship? In general, women are the relationship "makers" or "breakers."

Obviously, this is unfair. Just because our culture socialized us this way does not mean we can't break out of those chains and create a different reality for ourselves. This starts with all you men out there taking equal responsibility for the health of your relationship.

Wood, J. (1993). Engendered relationships: Interaction, caring, power, and responsibility in close relationships. In S. Duck (Ed.), *Processes in close relationships Contexts of close relationships. (Vol. 3, pp. 26-54). Beverly Hills: Sage.*

Kirkpatrick, L. & Davis, K. (1994). Attachment style, gender, and relationship stability: A longitudinal analysis. Journal of Personality and Social Psychology, 66, 502- 512.

Relationship Monitoring

It is common for people in relationships to secretly test their partner to assess the extent of his/her love. While both sexes do this, they approach the tests differently. For example, women are more secretive about it than men. This is due to the fact that women are overall more attentive to the relational process. As a result, they consciously process the partnership more than men. Therefore, this means that men are more likely to unconsciously test their lover's commitment.

There are three general areas in which relationships are monitored and tested.* The first is partner "endurance." This measures how well your mate will stand up to costly criticism. For example, if you can't stand how messy or lazy your partner is, you are likely to complain about it. The more complaining you do, the more likely it is that your partner will either pull away or run away. But, the longer they stay, the better they are passing the partner "endurance" test.

The second area people monitor their relationship is in partner trustworthiness. In other words, will their mate respond to someone who flirts with him/her? In theory, the more a person "resists temptation" from outsiders, the more they love their present mate.

And third, people test partner commitment. For example, how will your partner react when you formally introduce them to your family and friends as your "boyfriend" or "girlfriend?" How will they respond if they are separated from you for an extended period of time?

It is important to remember that all of these areas of relationship monitoring are born out of fear. The more you "test" your relationship, the weaker you become as an individual and as a couple. Do some inner work so you don't have to test your lover. Project confidence and love and enjoy the ride.

Baxter, L.A. & Wilmot, W.W. (1984). Secret tests: Social strategies for acquiring information about the state of the relationship. Human Communication Research, 11, 171-201.

Ingredients for Romance & Intimacy

There are a number of variables that differentiate romantic relationships from platonic ones. According to Robert Sternberg, three ingredients are necessary to nurture a romantic relationship. * If all of these are not present or one or two areas are weak, the health of the relationship will suffer greatly.

The first ingredient is commitment. There must be at least an expectation of relationship permanence (or expected to be at some point in the future). There must be the intention to remain in the relationship even if conflict occurs. Second, passion must exist. Passion can be defined as intensely positive feelings of attraction that increase your desire to be with another person. Finally, intimacy must be present, which is a sustained feeling of closeness or connection. This feeling must exist on both an emotional and a physical level.

Schaefer and Olson go even further to define intimacy: they posit five distinct aspects.* The following are the results of their research:

Emotional Intimacy: Reflects the ability and comfort with communicating openly about feelings and emotions.

Social Intimacy: Reflects the couple's closeness with mutual friends and social networks.

Sexual Intimacy: Reflects physical closeness.

Intellectual Intimacy: Reflects the fact that partners are able to talk about a wide range of issues with each other.

Recreational Intimacy: Reflects the common interests in leisurely activities between the partners.

Now that you are familiar with the ingredients that need go into a healthy relationship, take some time to rate yours. Do you see eye-to-eye with your partner on all levels? Which areas need work? What can you do to make sure that you increase your levels of intimacy? As with anything, improvement takes work. Both of you must put in equal effort in order to achieve measurable success.

Sternberg, R.J. (1986). A triangular theory of love. Psychological Review, 93, 119-135.

Schaefer, M. & Olson, D. (1981). Assessing intimacy: The PAIR inventory. Journal of Marriage and Family Therapy, 7, 47-60.

Interpersonal Power

Power and interpersonal influence are intimately intertwined. You cannot effectively persuade another person if you don't possess some sort of "power." In relationships, the use of power can cause problems.

The reason for this is because the word "power" has a negative connotation in our culture. People perceive it to mean power "over" someone else or taking away someone else's power. This is not necessarily true. While there are many people who abuse their power, it can also be used for positive things. Or, it can be completely neutral. It all depends on the intention of the person who possesses it.

The other interesting thing about power is that it depends on the relationship between you and another person. It varies from situation to situation. You may have more power than your partner in one situation but not in another. In many relationships, it shifts back and forth between partners, which is actually a healthy model to follow. If it doesn't, the relationship is thrown off balance.

All of these kinds of power manifest in different ways. You can be "strategically nice," intimidate, self-promote, or act helpless to get what you desire from your partner. Whatever you use, it influences the overall quality of your relationship.

Take some time to consider what power you use the most with your partner. Are you being effective? Is he/she taking advantage of you? Are you taking advantage of them? If you analyze where you stand in relation to your power, you can more accurately assess your relationship and how to improve it. Always remember, don't abuse your power or it will come back to get you—either in this lifetime or another one.

Use the "Test of Publicity"

Usually, people think their behavior is quite acceptable. In fact, if and when their partner points out that something they are doing is unacceptable to him/her, they frequently react with shock and denial. They think, "How could he possibly say I'm that bad? Look at him!" In other words, people quickly "turn the tables," so to speak, and point the finger back at their mate.

In other repairs in this book, we speak of responsibility for your actions. Let's start with that concept: take responsibility for what you do (and don't do). If you ever have any question of whether or not something you are doing (or not doing) is acceptable to your partner, you can take this easy test.

Simply speaking, the "Test of Publicity" says: don't do anything that you wouldn't want the whole world to know about. For example, we might say, "If I flirt with this person, it could get back to everyone I know, so I won't do it." Or, if you don't know if you should put something on your resume, think, "Would I be embarrassed if other people found out about this?" The "Test of Publicity" means never doing anything you wouldn't tell the whole world.

Now, let's apply this to your relationship with an example. Perhaps, you (or your partner) are the kind of person who usually doesn't help out a lot around the house or with the children. Would you be proud of this behavior if your partner went and told your mother, father, friends, and co-workers? Probably not.

Every time you take an action in your relationship, subject it to the "Test of Publicity." If you wouldn't announce it to the whole world, you probably shouldn't do it.

RADICAL TIPS

FOR MAINTENANCE & REPAIR

The tips in this sub-section of "Maintenance & Repair" are **RADICAL**

You will need an open mind and a curious spirit (or at least a sense of humor) to read these tips!

Extramarital Affair Triangle

An affair can calm the anxious partner but end up being an avoidance tactic to keep from dealing with the dysfunctional marriage/union. When the affair comes out, conflict will center upon the affair and further displace the real issue.

The affair itself is a three-people triangle. There may be others in the relationship. Maybe fighting has caused one of the partners to lean toward their family, or a child, or friends, which creates another triangle.

Big questions need to be answered. One partner had the affair, but both are responsible for the atmosphere that launched it. Both partners need to take responsibility. What did the aggrieved partner do to help drain the relationship of passion? Explore joint responsibility for the state of the union. Explore the needs that were/are being fulfilled by the affair.

What is the partner having the affair willing to do? Will they give up their lover? Do they want to end the marriage/union? Maybe they refuse to do anything while continuing the affair. Who desires a separation? Is the partner having the affair willing to not see their partner or their lover during the separation? This may help to resolve the confusion, but, statistically, those in this position often move toward their lover.

If you are the aggrieved partner, be emotionally neutral toward your partner. No berating, no threats, no begging them to come back.

If both partners desire to save the marriage, reestablishing trust is critical to the process. It will take a partnership effort. There may be other interlocking triangles besides the outside lover. The bereaved partner may have created a triangle with a close friend, family member, or the children of the union. These triangles need to be explored, and, together, you will have to find strategies for dealing with them. It will take time, but it can be done. Start doing enjoyable things together and avoid criticism, blame, and judgment. Forgiveness is key to reestablishing your union.

Uncover Past Life Ties to Your Partner

Reincarnation is the spiritual philosophy that our spirits are "re-born" into new bodies in different time periods. The chief purpose of this process of birth and re-birth is education. This does not mean education of our minds and bodies but the education of our souls.

For instance, consider our physical life in comparison to our soul life. We are born into this world with no knowledge. As we grow and develop, we learn about the world. We are educated through formal schooling as well as through life experiences. By the time we are old and ready to pass on, we are much wiser and more knowledgeable than we were when we were born. The same is true for the soul. Each lifetime of the soul can be compared to a stage in a human being's life. The soul is constantly growing, learning, and evolving. Each lifetime on earth provides more opportunity for advancement.

We are constantly challenged to grow in our relationships. Other people test our limits. Our associations with them give us great joy and sorrow. Therefore, we have ample opportunity for learning.

Your problems with your mate may be rooted in the past lives you have shared. Every thought, deed, and action creates karma. Unfortunately, most of the karma we have created has been negative. That is why you are with your partner in this life—to work out problems from lifetimes past.

You can gain answers from getting a past life regression by seeing a hypnotherapist or using a CD. You can uncover any negativity that you and your partner share and start to let go of the past and work it out. The information you can receive from this experience is incredibly valuable. You will be able to make positive changes once you find out that your problems stem from other lives.

Balance Your Male/ Female Energy Ratio

Couples need the right mixture of male/female energy to have a successful relationship. As individuals, we all have different ratios. Similar to the yin/yang concept, opposites make a whole and balance each other out.

A good analogy would be when a cook is making a dish. This person would have to get the recipe just right. For example, if chocolate chip cookies are being made, to use 2 cups of salt and 2 teaspoons of sugar would not make the cookies taste very good. It would make the ratio out of balance, and the result would be distasteful. The same is true for relationships.

Most women have more female than male energy. The same is true for men (more male than female energy). However, each person is an individual and has their own unique blend. A man who is very assertive, dominant, and outspoken would have excessive male energy. A woman who is very nurturing, loving, and submissive would have excessive female energy. If these two people were in a relationship together, the balance of energy may be good because they complement each other. However, if suddenly the woman became more independent and outspoken (male energy), the energy balance would be thrown off, and, as a result, the male may feel threatened. Consequently, the relationship could suffer.

Some people's energy balances each other's out well. However, most don't. That is why most relationships do not thrive. Therefore, it is important to learn what you can do about it.

In order to balance out your male/female energy (both at an individual and relationship level), you must strive to be androgynous with your behaviors. Androgyny refers to having equal amounts of male and female behaviors. It makes people more empathic. The more empathic a person is, the more they understand another person's point of view. Empathy is key to a successful relationship.

Sexual Morality?

Sexual mores have swung like a pendulum back and forth throughout history. In twelfth century England, thinking of sex was considered a sin, even if you were married. The "missionary" position was the only acceptable coitus position and only for the purpose of begetting children. Sex was totally forbidden on Sundays, Wednesdays, Fridays, and for 40 days before Christmas or Easter. Any pleasure experienced from this regrettably necessary act of perpetuating the race was also considered a sin.

Between the years 800 and 1000 in England, celibacy was considered unhealthy, and prostitution was supported by authorities. Public nudity was accepted at beaches, and women were free to take lovers regardless of their marital status.

The Inquisition, which began as a battle against heresy, eroded into a battle against sex. Many a woman lost her life because a man accused her of causing his impotence.

Ancient Sparta encouraged male and female public nudity. Young people experienced considerable sexual freedom before marriage, as celibacy was considered a crime. It was acceptable for older men to "loan" their wives to relatives or friends for the purpose of bearing a child if the combination might result in a superior human specimen.

We could share hundreds of examples of sexual extremes that have resulted in sexual confusion. Our souls have been programmed by our past lives, so we have innate feelings about what is right and wrong for us. Depending upon our past programming, our sexual orientation may or may not be compatible with society's current mores.

Problems arise out of sexual repression. If you question your sexual proclivities, you need to ask yourself, "Does what I do sexually work for me? Does it manifest love, health, happiness, aliveness and allow me full self-expression?" If it does, and no one else is harmed by your practices, it would be ill-advised to be concerned with society's ideas of right and wrong.

Feng Shui Your House

Have you ever walked into an environment and felt either fantastic or awful? If so, you were experiencing Feng Shui, which is the study of how energy flows in an environment. It is an ancient practice that originated with the Chinese and has been formally utilized for about 3,000 years.

Our relationship with our surroundings is interactive; the health of one is reflected in the other. Just as we are molded by the people who rear us, we are shaped by the sensory interactions between us and our environment. On a subconscious level, our setting triggers an automatic response.

According to the philosophy of Feng Shui, we can orchestrate our fate by manipulating our environment. We can identify conditions in a living space that affect us either in positive or negative ways. The goal is to create environments that can add to all areas of your life—including your relationships.

The Chinese have identified the parts of a room where specific human experiences thrive. Some areas represent career, money, or relationships, just to name a few. The Ba Gua is an octagon shape that identifies optimum locations for different activities. It is based on the idea that right and left have inherent meaning for human beings. Right controls emotions and abstract thinking, and the left handles critical thinking. The following is how the Ba Gua is set up: **1|** the center of a room represents health, **2|** the right side of a room: relationships, descendents, and compassion, **3|** the left: power, community, and wisdom, **4|** the top: future, and (5) the bottom: self.

You can place certain things in the "relationship" corner of the rooms in your house to enhance your relationship. For example, a plant represents growth, so you might want to put one in that corner to symbolize the healthy growth of your relationship. You can set up your environment so it supports the improving of your relationship.

Empaths

An empath is very sensitive to the thoughts of others. They may be overly aware of other people's moods and feelings. They might even be able to predict what someone is going to say before they say it. For example, if someone they work with becomes depressed, they might start feeling blue themselves without knowing why.

In his book *Past Lives, Future Loves*, Dick discusses a case history in which this kind of empathy caused a marriage to dissolve. A man named Owen was an empath. He was easily subjected to other people's mental input that he mistakenly thought was his own. While he knew he was sensitive to others, he didn't realize the disastrous consequences it could have on his own life. He says, "I've messed up my marriage by messing around with about six different lovely ladies. This also meant losing my kid. I screwed up at work because my marriage became such a scene I couldn't concentrate on what I was supposed to be doing." (p. 69)

There was one woman in particular who he found himself attracted to, and vice versa. In order to explain their affair, Dick explains, "Everyone has a medically measurable brain wave, and tests have proven that two people who have close brain waves, or exactly the same brain waves, will experience a higher degree of ESP with each other than others....[it is probable that] Alison is a highly sexual person and could have been transmitting her own sexual desires and fantasies to Owen. If she was fantasizing having sex with him while masturbating, although he was miles away, he could have mentally picked up sexual desires that he perceived to be his own. The result was additional extramarital involvement."

If drastic personality or mood changes are a problem in your relationship, you might want to psychically protect yourself (and your partner) from the thought transference of others.

Release Sexual Pressure

If your sexual drive is out of synch with your partner, know that arousal is most likely when the less desiring partner is more receptive, and when they are free to choose if they want sex or not. Fun as it may be, sex does not need to be spontaneous. In our world of over-commitment and multi-tasking, odds are against both partners being emotionally receptive and physically available at the same time.

How about planning for sex? "Tonight at eight, let's both kick back with a glass of wine." This puts sex on both partner's "to do" list. But, at the same time, it creates an obligation to have sex, and, if sex is obligatory, anxiety may result, killing desire. So, we have a paradox that needs to be resolved.

Here's an idea: once you both agree to when and where, you also agree you're not necessarily committing to intercourse, and you will each be responsible for your own sexual release. You both have total freedom as to how you "get off," if you decide to get off at all. You may choose to have intercourse, but there are many other ways to resolve sexual tension. One of you may massage the other (a welcome experience if not accompanied by expectations.) Side-by-side masturbation can be a freeing experience. Or, masturbate each other. Or, have oral sex. Or, the one most desiring sex masturbates while their partner watches and provides verbal encouragement. Be creative. Play naked in the back seat of the car. Any sexual expression may naturally lead to intercourse, but both partners must be free to say no. Move past feeling shameful about masturbation. If everyone does it (and everyone does, married or not), make it all right to express this intimacy in front of your partner. It will become a turn-on. The goal of planning a "sex date" is to become more relaxed about sexual issues.

Harness the Power of the Law of Attraction

Your relationship isn't bad because your partner won't do the dishes, or because they are not romantic anymore, or because they don't listen when you talk; rather, it's how you feel about these things that causes your problems. This is called the Law of Attraction.

The Law of Attraction is a basic rule of physics that has been scientifically proven. Simply stated: like attracts like. We "get back" what we "put out." This universal law is based on the fact that we are all energy. Us, you, the table, and the blade of grass—everything is made up of energy, and all energy vibrates at a different rate.

The most powerful energy/vibrations that we emit are in the form of our emotions. In fact, we are like a walking magnet. We attract other emotions that are on the same wavelength as the ones we are "putting out." For example, I'm sure you would admit that it is much easier to be nice and loving to your partner when they are nice and loving toward you. If he/she is being negative towards you, you most likely reciprocate with more negative emotion. Your good or bad emotions elicit the same from your partner. As you can see, this is "like attracts like," or the Law of Attraction in action.

What should you do about it? It all starts with awareness. You must consciously analyze the emotions you "put out" every day toward your partner and count how many of them are positive and how many are negative. If you are heavy on the negative side, you need to make some radical adjustments to your thinking.

Controlling your thoughts and emotions toward your partner is difficult, but it can be done. It takes constant attention and practice, but it will be worth it.

Sex & The Law of Magnetism

The Law of Magnetism says you draw to you what you "put out." While it applies to many areas of your life, you can use it to improve your sex life. First, you have to analyze the magnetic nature of your sexual energy.

If you don't love yourself or think you are attractive/sexy, no one else will. Not even your partner. Perhaps, when you met, you felt more desirable, but, as time went on, you lost that feeling. Loving yourself and seeing yourself as sexy are very clear vibrations that are sent out to others. It is a sexually stimulating frequency that sends the message, "I love myself. I am attractive. I am worthy of sexual desire from others." People "pick up" that you know you deserve an exciting sexual relationship.

It's important to examine your beliefs about sex, because these are at the core of the vibrations you send out. Perhaps, it has little to do with how you feel about yourself but with how you were raised. Many religions discourage sex and/or make people feel "dirty" or "bad" if they have sexual encounters or thoughts. These beliefs are fear-based that block you from experiencing a fulfilling sexual relationship.

All of your thoughts compose your personal energy field. This is a very real thing; it can be photographed. Many people refer to it as your "aura," and it contains your positive and negative beliefs about sexuality. Negative energy draws more negative sexual circumstances, and positive energy draws the opposite.

If you want to improve your sex life, analyze your thoughts about sex in general and about yourself in particular, "Do you see yourself as a sexual person? Do you think it's normal to enjoy sex and safe to have sex? Do you love your body and feel in control of your sexuality?" These are just a few questions to get you started.

Creative Visualization

You can use your imagination to create the relationship you desire. This process is called creative visualization. Even though this might sound rather mysterious, it isn't. It is something you do unconsciously every day. Your imagination is the creative force of the Universe. Without imagination, nothing would come into existence.

Unfortunately, humans are mostly programmed with negativity; they automatically think in terms of "lack." However, the Universe is abundant. All you need to do in order to get results is believe this to be true and harness your imagination in a positive direction. You can learn to focus your creative energy to mold a good relationship.

First, try going into a relaxed, meditative state, and mentally imagine the two of you in a happy, content, satisfied state of being. Conjure up a feeling of it being true, or at least that it is possible, as well as the fact that it is "already happening." It is important to imagine it as existing now because the subconscious mind will start working to bring it to fruition.

Besides this simple exercise, there are many other types of strategies you can use to put your imagination to work. You can write affirmations, "stories," or make collages, just to name a few. Whatever you do, it is important to repeat it several times a day. This focuses your energy and imagination toward your goal and helps bring it into existence.

If you are truly sincere in your desire and have the right intentions, soon you will find yourself in a relationship that is easier more free-flowing. Your partner might be easier to get along with and more pleasant to be around. Eventually, you will find that positive changes are almost magically occurring without much more effort than your ability to daydream it into reality.

Create Your Own Reality

Humans are programmed to think that reality is outside of their control. They think they are "victims" and at the mercy of other people and outside circumstances. This could not be farther from the truth.

Everything that exists in the physical world began as a thought. Before Thomas Edison invented the light bulb, he had to imagine it. He had to have the idea first. The same is true for your life. Your job, your house, and your relationships all began because of an original thought. You thought about it, you wanted it, and thus, you created it. You have even created things that you did not want, simply by thinking about the possibility of it happening. Granted, you might not know how you did that. However, it does not change the fact that it happened.

Your thoughts are incredibly powerful. They have the power to create. They have the power to destroy. They have so much more power than you ever thought possible.

Therefore, the combination of your and your partner's thoughts are what created the state of your relationship. Yes, you both have taken actions that helped it along, but the thoughts preceded the actions.

Since you created the relationship, you also have the power to change it. You can harness the power of your imagination in order to make it more positive. There are many ways you can do this. For example, you can daydream it into existence. If you want your partner to be more attentive, romantic, and loving, imagine that he/she already is. In your mind's eye, ***see*** him bringing you flowers, holding your hand, and cooking you romantic dinners. Make it ***real***. But above all, ***believe*** it can happen. ***Know*** it can happen.

There are lots of creative yet simple actions you can take to improve your relationship. All you need to do is focus on positive thoughts, sit back, and watch it change for the better.

Investigate Your Parallel Lives

The relationship problems you are currently experiencing may not be your fault. And they may not even be your partner's fault. Perhaps you can blame them on one or more of your parallel lives.

A parallel life is a difficult concept to grasp. Similar to reincarnation, your soul inhabits other bodies. However, unlike reincarnation, this phenomenon happens during the same time period. With reincarnation, a soul is only one person at a time. With parallel lives, a soul can be many people at the same time. The soul is exploring several different lives at the same time as different people.

For example, let's say you are Jane Smith, a 36-year-old woman living in Seattle in 2007. But you may also be 69 year-old Robert Adams living in Sydney, Australia, 53 year-old Beatrice Henthorne living in London, England, and 12 year-old Yung-Soo Xi living in Singapore. And all of these lives are taking place at the same time, right here in the year 2007.

As people who have investigated parallel lives, most people find that they are living approximately three or four different lives at the same time. The purpose of this is similar to that of reincarnation. Each lifetime as a different human provides opportunity for new learning, whether it took place in 3202 B.C. or in the year 2007.

All of your parallel lives are connected and influence each other on an unconscious level. Let's say that 53 year-old Beatrice Henthorne is being physically abused by her new boyfriend. This is causing her deep emotional turmoil, and she doesn't know how to rectify the situation. Her negative energy could be affecting your relationship. Therefore, it has nothing to do with what you or your partner have been doing, but everything to do what Beatrice and her new boyfriend are going through.

Therefore, it is beneficial to investigate your parallel lives to see if their negativity is bleeding through into your life. Once you receive such awareness, it will be easier to put your relationship "problems" into perspective and move forward.

SECTION THREE

Letting Go & Moving On

Table of Contents

SECTION THREE TIPS FOR LETTING GO & MOVING ON

You Are Free to Start Over . . . 130
Invoke the Law of Forgiveness . . . 131
Examine and Improve Your Self-Worth . . . 132
Figure Out What You Really Want . . . 134
Start Over or Let Go . . . 135
Ending Detachment Process . . . 136
Stop Asking "Why?" . . . 137
Find Balance . . . 138
Insecurity . . . 139
Monitor & Change Your Self-Talk . . . 140
Find & Keep Inner Peace . . . 141
Choose Growth . . . 142
Analyze Your Belief System . . . 143
Beyond Repair . . . 144
Live Dangerously . . . 145
Relationships Do Not Work . . . 146
He Who Trembles . . . 147
Everything That Surrounds You . . . 148
Seek Security Within . . . 149
Let Go . . . 150
Avoid Comparisons . . . 151
Start Living . . . 152
Let Your Spirit Lead . . . 153
Use Mind Programming . . . 154
Controlling Outcomes . . . 155
A Path With A Heart . . . 156
Swimming in Circles . . . 157
Behavior vs. Feelings . . . 158
Love Yourself . . . 159
Affirmations . . . 160
The Spiritual Connection . . . 161
Invoke the Law of Desire . . . 162
Grieve . . . 163
Depression . . . 164
"Why?" . . . 166
Desirelessness . . . 168
Join an Online Dating Service . . . 169
Follow Your Intuition, Not Your Logic . . . 170
Don't Compromise This Time . . . 171
Don't Be Desperate . . . 172
Be Patient . . . 173
Negotiate Boundaries . . . 174
Write Down Your Future Partner's Qualities . . . 175
Beware of "Good Interviewers" . . . 177
"Dater" or "Relationship Person"? . . . 178
Know What You Want Right Now . . . 179
Go With The Flow . . . 180
Don't Forget to Pause . . . 181
Don't Care About What Other People Think . . . 182
Embrace Risk . . . 183
Welcome the New Beginning . . . 184
Don't Worry About Your Age . . . 185
Seek Awareness of Your Truth . . . 186
Being Single: Problem or Opportunity? . . . 187
Leave Your Options Open . . . 188
Don't Let Charm Blind You . . . 189
Examine Your Self-Worth . . . 190
Live in the Present . . . 191

Insecurity is a State of Mind 192
Fight Jealousy.................... 193
Reserve Judgment 194
Independent or Dependent?......... 195
Let it Fizzle 196
Don't Commit Too Soon............. 197
Don't Encourage "Stalkers" 198
Take a Break 199

RADICAL TIPS FOR LETTING GO & MOVING ON

Investigate You Future Lives.......... 202
Make Contact with Your Future Self............... 204
Awareness of "Soul-Switching"....... 205
Use Automatic Writing to Find Answers 206
Investigate Your Destiny 208
Protect Yourself From Psychic Attacks............... 209
Taking A Lover 210
The Law of Resistance.............. 211
Belief Blocks..................... 212
Write a Thank You Letter to the Universe (The Law of Gratitude) 213

This section is for people who are:

1. Thinking about getting out of a relationship

or

2. Have just gotten out of a relationship and need to emotionally let go

or

3. Need some tips to create a better relationship next time

You Are Free To Start Over

You are always free to start over. When something is not working, you can decide to stop playing. If you are experiencing friction or feeling resentment, your soul may be calling for you to end this — so you can start something else.

This does not mean that you cannot succeed, but your soul may be telling you that the direction you are going is not taking you where you want to be. By admitting that an aspect of your life is not working, you are free to begin moving in a new direction that will work.

Before deciding to start over, you may want to explore any personal fears that are motivating the need to begin again. Resentment is a fear-based emotion based upon you wanting someone else to be the way you want them to be. Is that justified? If you are holding on to a past hurt, the other person is keeping you a prisoner in the here and now.

Assuming you can release any fear-based emotions (especially blame) relating to your wanting to start over, the best place to begin self-processing is to explore what is true for you. Is being true to yourself more important than your fear of consequences? When you are not true to yourself you are living in fear.

You do not want to live in fear of what others might think about you starting over.

Once you have decided to start over, it will be time to stop explaining yourself to other people. It is your right to offer no excuses or justifications for your decisions or behavior. You may want to explain why you have acted in a particular way to those with whom you share a close relationship, but you do not owe anyone an explanation. Excuses and explanations weaken your position.

To start over means leaving behind your old ideas about yourself.

Invoke the Law of Forgiveness

Forgiveness is key to creating the relationship you desire. You need to give up pain, anger, resentment, and fear to make it happen. Negative energy associated with non-forgiveness will plug up the channel for positive energy and block you from getting what you want.

Many people think that if they forgive someone, they are "accepting" what the person did. This is not true. In order to truly forgive, try viewing it as a selfish act. Forgiveness is much easier to carry around than anger and resentment. When you rid yourself of negative emotions about your partner, you will feel so much freer and lighter and will be able to manifest a more positive relationship, either with this one or in the future.

You must forgive yourself. We've all done things we regret in relationships, but it's in the past, so move on. It is doing you no good to hold on to the guilt.

The mere act of forgiveness is a cleansing of negative energy between two people. However, it's not enough to say, "I forgive John." You must feel it on every level of your body and mind. If you know that forgiveness is selfish, why not do it. What's holding you back?

Non-forgiveness ties you to your present or past partners in a negative way. When you forgive, the other person is affected positively too, even if they don't know you forgave them.

How can you begin the process of forgiveness? Realize everyone is fallible—we all make mistakes and are a product of our experiences. What your partner did "to you" is more a sign of their weakness than of your lack of value. Be compassionate towards them. This will re-frame forgiveness so you can truly release the negative energy needed to improve your relationship.

Examine and Improve Your Self-Worth

Examine your feelings of self-worth. High self-esteem is critical to a happy relationship. If you have an unhappy union, perhaps it is because you do not feel worthy of having it otherwise. We only attract what we feel we deserve. If you created an imperfect relationship currently (or in the past), it probably has more to do with your inner self than it does your partner.

We are all living expressions of our belief system, which was created by past programming. Through all our lives, our brain has been programmed with thoughts and ideas about how the world works. In fact, even when you were in your mother's womb, you were hearing messages from the outside world. If your parents talked about how they didn't want to have a baby, that message was recorded on your brain and could have translated into, "I'm not wanted." While that is an extreme example, we all have messages sent to us by parents, siblings, peers, teachers, and the media. If you received negative messages about yourself, it is likely that it has affected the quality of your romantic relationships.

Your beliefs generate the thoughts and emotions that create all of your experiences. Thinking you are "not good enough" will create feelings of possessiveness, jealously, and resentment in any of your relationships. Projecting these will only hurt you and your mate. It will make you unpleasant to be around, and the negative energy surrounding you will make your partner uneasy.

You cannot change what you don't recognize. The first step to a new image of high self-worth can be analyzing how you feel about yourself. Explore how many of your feelings are the result of past programming. The old feelings have nothing to do with who you actually are. With this awareness, it will be easier to release the past and embrace new feelings of self-worth.

Also, understand that self-esteem is the result of what you do in life. When you act in ways that make you feel good about yourself, you increase your self-esteem. As a bottom line in life, never do anything that will cause you to lose self-esteem.

Figure Out What You Really Want

This sounds easy. After all, who doesn't know what they want? Well, the answer is: most people. They think they know what they want, but when it comes right down to it, they don't.

Instead of figuring out what they want, most people spend their time complaining about what they don't want. A woman might say, "I wish my husband wouldn't watch so much sports. I feel like he ignores me." From hearing that, it would be natural to conclude that she wants him to stop watching sports and spend more time with her. However, when he does that, she discovers that she doesn't have the time to do other things on her own, such as a pastime she loves.

So, even though we think we want something, when we actually get it, it might not be what we want. Therefore, you have to spend time thinking about what the outcome would be if you actually got it. What would you have to give up? Would you actually like the relationship better? There is usually a "pay off" for keeping our lives the way they are. What is yours?

To figure out what you do want, start with writing a "Don't Want" list. Write down all the things you don't like about your partner and the relationship. Then, turn that "Don't Want" list into a "Want" list. If you don't want this, then you must want the opposite of this. The next step is to spend quality time asking yourself if you really do want the opposite?

Regardless of whether you are currently in a relationship or will be in the future, you must communicate your wants to your partner. None of us are mind readers. We actually have to hear a message for it to be understood. If you and your mate spend time sharing your want lists, you will come to realize how you can meet each other's needs.

Start Over or Let Go

Many people say they want to "start over." However, is it really possible to start over in relationships? If you have two people in the same relationship for twenty years, is it really possible to "erase the past" and begin anew? In reality, it's not possible to erase the past; however, we must forgive the past. We must commit to becoming new and improved people from this moment on.

Whether you are still in a relationship or just got out of one, there is a way you can start over. You can do it by adopting a new attitude toward the relationship or life in general. Whether it is only you or both of you, this simple action will help.

Most people are scared of new beginnings. You probably know people who constantly complain about their job, their partner, or anything and everything else. These people do not have the mindset of "nothing ventured, nothing gained." They feel safe where they are in the moment. However, no one is going to improve their relationship (or anything for that matter) if they don't take action to start over.

People don't strive for new beginnings because of fear. The unknown is scary. Even though we may not like where we are at the moment, it is still familiar, comfortable, predictable, and requires minimal effort. In theory, this sounds great. However, humans have a love/hate relationship with the familiar, the comfortable, and the predictable. There is a constant tension between wanting predictability and novelty. Once our relationship (or life) gets too predictable, we get bored and dissatisfied. But if our life is too exciting, it can become uncomfortable.

If you're unhappy with your relationship (or lack thereof), change it! Use every suggestion offered here to adopt a new attitude. It is may be difficult and scary, but that's what makes life interesting!

Ending Detachment Process

This is a behavior modification technique to accelerate emotional detachment. Be sure you want what you ask for. Then, write at least a dozen sentences that express your fears. Let's assume you realize your relationship with your husband has come to an end, but you fear having to experience all the pain of letting go and starting over again. Each sentence expresses a fear and is followed by another sentence that begins with STOP. This second sentence is then tape recorded with emotion. Here's how it works:

You say out loud, "I need John to survive mentally and physically." Then you press "play" on the tape recorder and hear, "STOP! John has already shown you how little her cares about your needs. You easily survive mentally and physically without him."

More examples: "Maybe there's still a chance that John and I can find a way to work things out." "STOP! You no longer deny the relationship is over. The two of you will now go your own ways. You accept what is."

"If John and I part, the pain will go on and on for a very long time." "STOP! If you and John part, you have the power and ability to sever the emotional ties with minimum attachment and create a happy, successful life without him."

"I don't know if I have the strength to start over." "STOP! You absolutely have the strength to start over. Starting over is far superior to tolerating a pain-filled life and repressing who you are."

INSTRUCTIONS Write out many more statements that cover all aspects of the relationship. Record only the "STOP" statements. Then verbally speak the first statement and immediately push play to hear the "STOP" statement. Repeat the statements 10 times and do the process three or four times a day. You don't have to induce an altered state of consciousness while running the process, but if you do, it will have much more programming power.

Stop Asking, "Why?"

When you ask, "Why did you do that?" you are attempting to put your partner on the defensive. The question is manipulative and, by asking it, you are showing a lack of awareness. You seek reasons, and reasons rarely exist. People always act emotionally. They invent logical reasons to justify their actions to themselves and others. Yet, the reasons are just rationales and excuses and rarely have much to do with the facts. The reasons don't really matter, and no one could possibly know what they are. They lie buried in the way the person views the world, which is the result of all their past programming (all their previous experiences in this life and all of their past lives.)

When you ask "why," you demonstrate your lack of awareness.

When you explain "why," in response to someone questioning you, you demonstrate your lack of awareness. You, also, give away your power and reduce your self-esteem. You do not need to explain yourself, unless you want to for your own reasons.

You do what you do because that's what you do. That's why. They do what they do because that's what they do ... and that's what is.

It is important to distinguish between "why" questions intended to take away your power and "why" questions intended to clarify. For example,

"Why didn't you call me last week? I waited home every night by the phone." This "why" question is intended to manipulate you into feeling guilty, which results in a loss of self-esteem.

"Why is it better to use olive oil than canola oil?" This "why" question is asking for clarification and is intended to increase understanding; thus, answering it would not involve any loss of self-esteem.

Find Balance

What images does the word "balance" invoke for you? For us, it's the yin/yang symbol, followed by the image of a tightrope walker, carrying a pole—he's never in perfect balance. He continually moves the pole up and down and shifts weight from the right to the left. A little too much movement in one direction is quickly balanced by shifting weight in the other direction. The walker is never really in perfect balance for more than a moment. If he were, he would fall.

Life is a tightrope and, like the tightrope walker, you will never be in balance for long. If you were to strive to avoid all extremes, you'd limit your life and would certainly generate anxiety. Do not use this thinking as an excuse to be overindulgent, but if that is what you need to do, you'll soon generate an opposite pull of the forces.

If you know you're badly out of balance, take action before your body/mind finds a way of doing it for you. But stop worrying about finding perfect balance. If you can replace yin behavior with positive challenge, do it. Instead of endangering your mental or physical health, find a way to generate the needed experience, but in a way that can serve you.

From the perspective of reincarnation, we swing back and forth through our lifetimes in an ongoing quest to attain balance. From this overview, good really isn't good, and bad isn't bad. They are not opposites in conflict but two harmonious aspects of the same thing.

Life seeks balance. There can be no winter without a spring, no life without death, and no happiness without sadness. If one aspect of your relationship swings out of balance, other aspects will change in an attempt to find balance.

Insecurity

With few exceptions, everything you say is to make yourself more important or to obtain sympathy. Both are expressions of insecurity.

Monitor yourself and listen to what others are saying. The exceptions will be statements of fact and legitimate questions, but that's about it. We all talk and talk and talk, because we are insecure.

Lajos Egri, author of "The Art of Creative Writing," talks about fear as the universal emotion responsible for man's survival, "It is paradoxical but true that hate or love, treachery or loyalty, spring from one and the same source—insecurity. Emotion then is a thousand-pronged weapon to safeguard our lives. It spells out for our survival the basic tenet of our experience, insecurity, and now it has become a truism that life would be impossible without that insecurity of which we are so mortally afraid. Insecurity gives impetus to inventors to safeguard our existence."

You are not alone in experiencing insecurity. Everyone else in the world is right there with you, but everyone hides it well. Human emotions are rooted in insecurity, which equals self-preservation. The desire to survive is our primary motivator.

Let's look at the paradox here. When we can obtain security, we quickly become bored because there is no longer any potential for adventure. We fight for security, but, in obtaining it, we lose the game. This is why so many marriages become boring. The initial love affair was an adventure, but, when it became institutionalized as marriage, the union becomes routine and mundane—secure, but dull and boring.

Life swings from the known to the unknown and back again. In the known, life tends to become dull and boring. Venturing into the unknown, you're insecure, but challenged, your heart beats faster, you experience aliveness, and you see things with new eyes. You are insecure. Embrace insecurity for the potential adventures it offers you.

Monitor & Change Your Self-Talk

Our self-concept is created through interaction with our world. Major influences on us are our parents, siblings, peers, teachers, and the media, just to name a few. Since our mind is like a computer, it can be programmed, for better or for worse. By the time you reach adulthood, your self-concept has been ingrained into your brain for many years.

People seldom think about how they feel about themselves. What kind of negative messages did you receive as a child? Perhaps, your parents told you that you never live up to your potential. In their minds, they were trying to help you achieve and go on to do great things in life. However, you may have internalized it as, "I'm lazy, and I'm never going to amount to anything." It is useful to analyze these kinds of messages to see how they are affecting you today.

While the outside world helped create your self-concept, self-talk supports and perpetuates it. Your subconscious mind is programmed by your thoughts. Therefore, what you think about yourself is critically important.

Negative self talk can affect your relationship. Perhaps, you've gained a few pounds, and you're depressed about it. As a result, you say to yourself, "I'm a big fat pig. How can my husband possibly be attracted to me anymore?" These thoughts create your experience. They will affect how you think, talk, and act, which, in turn, will affect your partner's reactions to you. If you become negative, it is likely he will too. Or even if your self-talk isn't resulting in your changed behavior, just sending out negative vibes may subconsciously push your partner away.

Think about how your self-talk may be affecting your relationship. If negative programming has been accepted by your subconscious mind, get rid of it.

Find & Keep Inner Peace

The word "peace" conjures up the feelings of tranquility. If you are at peace, it probably means nothing bad is going on in your life, or you're effectively dealing with outside circumstances. In order to change your relationship for the better, you will be well served by finding and maintaining inner peace at all times. Inner peace gives you the power to express unconditional love.

We define "inner peace" as "letting go." Let go of your expectations in regard to how things turn out, or for your partner to be a particular way. Let go of the need to be right. Instead of butting heads and letting defensiveness get the best of you, control your reactions to outside circumstances.

In order to find and keep that inner peace, you must first know what it feels like. Few people are really peaceful. They run through life in a hurried frenzy and forget to stay calm and centered — probably because they don't know how. No one can really tell you what it feels like because you have to experience it for yourself. But you'll know it, when you feel it. It feels like you're not being affected by the outer world; instead, you're affecting the outer world with your inner peace. When you achieve inner peace, you will radiate it and have a positive influence on those in your circle.

Inner peace means acting rather than reacting. You need to reach deep within yourself, get in touch with your emotions, keep them in check, and think before you speak. If you find inner peace before you act or speak, you will find that your relationship, and, thus, your reality will become a better place.

Choose Growth

Many of us have nagging twinges of discontent in our lives, especially in our relationships. We want things to change, but we either do not know how to change them or just aren't ready to act. Sometimes people choose to ignore these twinges of discontent, and nothing is done. When nothing is done, there is no growth. Without growth, we become stagnant.

Energy cannot die; it can only transform. It either moves forward or backward. It cannot stand still. The same is true for our relationships. They are either moving forward with positive aliveness, or they are slowing down, stagnating, and moving backwards into negative aliveness. Eventually, the negative aliveness kills the relationship—or at very best, transforms it into something else.

We must have growth to live, but that does not mean that all growth is easy or enjoyable. In fact, much of it is exactly the opposite. You need to commit to learning from your "mistakes."

We learn about what we want from experiencing what we don't want. We learn about what does work by finding out what doesn't work. You must believe that every bad relationship you've ever had has made you a better person (including the one you're currently in). By drawing upon your experiences, you can discover your true needs.

Don't view your relationship issues as "problems." When you do, you usually complain and worry and verbalize them over and over. The more you talk about your problems, the more you program negative thinking into your subconscious mind. In the long run, it just further complicates the situation.

Instead, you need to view your relationship issues as growth opportunities. The main difference between people who have successful relationships and those who don't, is attitude. Attitude is the difference between the high achievers in life and all the others. Take some time to think about how you can grow in your relationship.

Analyze Your Belief System

Every experience you have ever had has influenced your belief system and your self-image. In order to investigate why you act the way you do in relationships, take a look into your past. Most of your answers will lie there.

First, take a look at your parents. Family provides our first social reality. They were your primary role models for a relationship. For better or for worse, we watched our parents and saw how they behaved. How did they express anger? Perhaps, they yelled and screamed at one another. Perhaps, you never saw them fight a day in your life. Either model is not productive. The first advocates the negative expression of emotion. The second advocates repressing anger. Both are equally destructive to a relationship.

Another less obvious example of where you can look in your past is to books and movies, especially the ones you consumed as a child. Fairytales are full of gender stereotypes and "happily-ever-after." Practically every woman would love to find her "Knight in Shining Armor." These themes of happy relationships even permeate our popular movies. These messages program our subconscious mind to desire a fantasy relationship. However, as we all know, this doesn't exist.

Analyzing your past can give you and your partner insight into each other. Even though it seems "we are who we are," your mind can change anything. Change begins with the acceptance of new beliefs. Your thoughts and emotions create your experiences. If you aren't happy with your relationship and want to change it, look at your belief system and how it was built throughout your life.

Disharmonious beliefs are like a cage that restricts your relationship potential and your life. Unfortunately, few people realize that they created their own cage. Decide which beliefs are working against you and change them. Freedom will follow.

Beyond Repair

Relationships will teach you, challenge you, and, sometimes, push you to your limits. You'll push back, testing your union, and conflicts will ensue between you and your mate. In response to this friction, you'll learn to resolve differences, or the differences will overwhelm you. If your partner is not the right person to accompany you through the next stages of your life, one of you will begin to withdraw. When this happens, you have probably learned all you can from each other. Even though it will appear that one of you is responsible for the ending, you both contributed to the dissolution. There should be no blame—wish each other well as you both move into the transformational phase.

If your relationship is beyond repair, accept that you could never have repaired your union by keeping it the way it was. If it is time to separate, consider redefining the term "repair." Do not think in terms of "fixing" what is.

The idea is not to stop having a relationship with your partner. A living-together or marital relationship may have to become a living-apart friendship. The other person may remain in your life, but in a different way.

As difficult as this may be to accept, work on it. The way you experience life is the result of the way you choose to view what happens to you. Your viewpoint is the deciding factor in whether you experience life lovingly or fearfully.

In most of the situations in our lives, we do not actually repair problems, except through viewpoint. By changing your viewpoint, you can eliminate the effects of a problem, so you are no longer affected by the problem. If you are no longer affected by a problem, you do not have a problem (even though nothing about the problem situation may have changed.)

Read that over a few times until the wisdom comes through. Then decide upon the viewpoint you choose to embrace.

Live Dangerously

"Live Dangerously" read a sign on Friedrich Nietzsche's wall.

Nietzsche was a German philosopher who taught that traditional values represented a "slave morality." His quest for personal liberation is associated with some New Age thinking today. He maintained that all human behavior is motivated by the will to power (the power over oneself that is necessary for creativity.) As role models for what Nietzsche called an "overman," he mentioned Socrates, Jesus, Leonardo da Vinci, Michelangelo, and Shakespeare.

When questioned about the "Live Dangerously" sign, Nietzsche claimed it was to remind him, "My fear is great."

Nietzsche advocated "letting go" and living life as a great adventure.

What about you? Your inner nature calls for you to quest and learn and grow.

"No," you say, "I want security. Aliveness is dangerous. I cannot follow my inner nature."

When you try to protect yourself from change to maintain security, more often than not, you'll experience a reduction in your life-force. Your soul will suffer. And, for what? Security isn't secure. Life always changes.

Living dangerously means when you're offered a choice, you take the growth choice (not the safe choice, the comfortable choice, or the socially acceptable choice.) You choose based upon what generates aliveness for you. The results will provide an opportunity to learn and grow.

The Universal Law of Growth says, deep within your center, you know what is best for you, and it will always be to strive for more awareness. Never allow yourself to reach a level of self-satisfaction where there is no new challenge. For most of us, there will be no new growth without the agitation of discontent. The idea is to carefully study your dissatisfactions, for they will tell you what you are about to leave behind and possibly point to a new future direction.

Relationships Do Not Work

Charlotte Joko Beck, in her book "Everyday Zen," claims relationships do not work, "There never was a relationship that worked."

Why? Because, with any relationship, we want something. There are expectations — some subtle, some not-so subtle. We try to figure out our relationships and try to find a way to make them work so we can get what we want. The problem is "wanting something" and the resulting expectations.

Beck says, "We often misinterpret what marriage is about. When a relationship isn't working, it means that the partners are preoccupied with 'I': 'What I want is ....' or 'This isn't right for me.' If there is little wanting, then the relationship is strong and it will function. That's all life is interested in. As a separate ego with your separate desires, you are of no importance to life. And all weak relationships reflect the fact that somebody wants something for himself or herself."

Beck uses a house analogy to make a point about rigidity in marriage and life. There are new designs for beach-front houses that protect the structure from the occasional big storms that flood such residences. In the new designs, when flooded, the middle of the house collapses and the water, instead of destroying the whole house, rushes through the middle and leaves the structure standing.

Flexibly structured relationships function in much the same way by absorbing shocks and stresses and continuing to function. When a relationship is based primarily on "I want" or "I demand," the structure is rigid and will be unable to withstand the pressures of life.

Life will test all relationships like a strong wind beating at the union. If the relationship can't take the beating, then it will have to grow stronger so it can take it, or the couple will be forced to part so that something new has an opportunity to arise from the ashes.

He Who Trembles

"Only to the extent that we expose ourselves over and over again to annihilation, can that which is indestructible arise within us. In this lies the dignity of daring. We must have the courage to face life, to encounter all that is most perilous in the world," said philosopher Karlfried Graf Durkeim.

In "Callings," Gregg LeVoy says, "The desire to protect ourselves from change probably does more harm to the flowing of human life and spirit than almost any other choice, but it is imperative to understand something about security: It isn't secure! Everything about security is contrary to the central fact of existence: Life changes. By trying to shelter ourselves from change, we isolate ourselves from living. By avoiding risk we may feel safe and secure (or at least experience a tolerable parody thereof--but we don't avoid the harangues of our consciences. It's almost axiomatic that the important risks we don't take now become the regrets we have later. In fact, I was once told that if I'm not failing regularly, I'm living so far below my potential that I'm failing anyway."

Osho says, "To accept the challenge of the unknown in spite of all fears, is courage. The fears are there, but if you go on accepting the challenge again and again, slowly, slowly those fears disappear, because the experience of the joy that the unknown brings, the great ecstasy that starts happening with the unknown makes you strong enough, gives you a certain integrity, makes your intelligence sharp. For the first time you start feeling that life is not just a boredom but an adventure. Then slowly, slowly fears disappear."

Your life will always mirror what you put out. Fearful thoughts and actions will generate a fearful life of NO action. When you hold back, your life holds back. When you're willing to be afraid and act anyway by committing yourself to life, you generate ALIVENESS and open to the full potential of JOY.

Everything That Surrounds You

Everything that surrounds you is an extension of you. Your mate, children, home, furniture, car, pets, yard, office, and career are all physical expressions of your belief system and attitudes. Your environment is a manifestation of your energy and core beliefs and expresses your self-image and cultural overview.

What mind has created, mind can change.

Change begins with the acceptance of new beliefs. Beliefs generate your thoughts and emotions, which create your experiences. If you aren't happy with your current life and want to change it, you need to change your core beliefs by allowing yourself to experience what you desire.

Your disharmonious beliefs are like a cage, restricting your potential and your life. If you want to escape from the cage, you must first recognize that it exists, and you're not free. You cannot change what you do not recognize. Sadly, most people are unaware they exist in a self-created prison.

What can you learn about yourself by examining your key life areas as an extension of you—a manifestation of your energy and core beliefs: Your mate? Your children? Your home? Your furniture? Your car? Your pets? Your yard? Your office? Your career?

Let's say, as an example, your yard and office are a mess. This may be a manifestation of a lack of control in your life. You would be well-served by cleaning up these areas as first steps of taking control of your life. Explore how this lack of control is reflected in other areas. What do you want? Begin mind programming with techniques that follow in the next example.

If your primary relationship no longer reflects who you are, explore your part in creating the way it is. Who have you become? Then consider what you desire to happen -be honest. Once you have clarity of intent, you can begin to program new beliefs in keeping with your desires.

Seek Security Within

Many people lack high self-esteem. If this is the case, it usually has a direct effect on your relationship. Because you are not secure with yourself, you look outside yourself to confirm you self worth. This seldom works.

The security you seek lies within. Do not look to your partner to boost your ego because we cannot have a happy, whole, relationship if we are not happy and whole within ourselves. You must see yourself as beautiful (both inside and out). You are a unique person, and you should learn to appreciate yourself.

When you are insecure, it turns people off. You are sending out a message to them saying, "I am not lovable. I don't think I'm lovable. But would you love me anyway?" Subconsciously, if your partner is receiving a negative message from you such as that, he or she might wonder why they should love you if you don't love yourself. Even though this may not happen overtly, the negative energy you give off might actually repel your partner.

Don't get lost in your false ego-self. Instead, you should search for your "real self." Who are you beyond your humanness? What makes you special? If you don't focus on these positive aspects, it is likely that you will become numb and perpetually lonely.

You don't want to be an energy vampire. Don't suck the energy from your partner. You want to add to their life, not subtract from it. If you are draining the life force out of your partner, change. If you don't, they will run in the opposite direction. Realize you need to do a lot of inner work before you work on the relationship.

Let Go

Even if you have tried everything you can, sometimes it isn't enough. Maybe you have used every possible strategy for relationship improvement and have followed all of the advice in this book, changed yourself, and become a better person. You've even tried to inspire change in your partner. But nothing has changed except you.

If this has happened, then it may be time to let go. You can only change yourself, not your partner. If only one person is working on the relationship, it will not work. Both people have to put in, not their "50%," but 100%. Each partner has to put forth equal effort in order for the relationship to survive.

If one mate works at the relationship, and the other doesn't, then it is like being in a relationship with a brick wall. You can stand there and talk to the brick wall, suggest change, and even have a conversation with it, but a brick wall will not change. It is what it is. If your partner is a brick wall, maybe it's time to move on. Don't think of leaving the relationship as "failure," but as taking very valuable lessons you can apply to a more fulfilling partnership.

Before you were born, you made a plan for your life, which involved meeting your partner for certain reasons. When the learning is complete, the Universe has other plans for you. Let go and go with the flow. The river knows its course, and it will lead you where you are supposed to be.

Letting go is never easy, but sometimes it is necessary. From a spiritual perspective, we must accept that there are aspects of our lives that are destined. Your soul chose the path a long time ago, "Destiny leads the willing. The rest, it drags." Isn't it better to be in the lead rather than being dragged?

Avoid Comparisons

Our culture socializes us to expect perfection or as close to it as we possibly can get. Because of this, many people compare their relationships to ideals that may not be possible for your particular relationship.

Comparisons can be made anywhere. Some people look to their parents' "perfect marriage" for the model they need to follow. Other people look to cultural examples, such as movies, televisions shows, or fairy tales. Where you look for the "ideal" is not important. What is important is that you recognize it and realize that every relationship is unique. You need to appreciate what you have.

Each person has their own set of experiences. You could have grown up in a big city while your partner grew up on a farm. Your family is extremely liberal and his is very conservative. You have a lot of friends, he has only a couple. You are very different people with different values and beliefs. When you come together with these very definite ways of seeing reality, the combination is truly unique.

Any time someone "tries to keep up with the Joneses" it just doesn't work. Don't compare yourselves to other relationships. If you do, don't think about how your relationship doesn't measure up, but instead how certain aspects of yours are superior.

If you must compare, choose a couple that embodies something positive. Evaluate them. Ask questions. See how you could incorporate some of their successes into your relationship. But approach it positively. Don't get down on yourself if you haven't achieved your goals. Stay strong and keep going and someday other people will look to your relationship as a role model.

Start Living

Are you living your best life and your best relationship? Or could you do better? People generally fall into one of the following categories: **1**| happy, **2**| content/satisfied, **3**| "just going through the motions"/stagnant, and **4**| unhappy. Unfortunately, not many are in the "happy" category. If you aren't either, you need to do something about it.

Humans get too comfortable in the familiar. What is familiar now probably used to be exciting, but now it has become predictable and will probably slip into being stagnant, and, eventually, you will end up unhappy. That is when you need to make the change.

Life is short. All of our days are numbered. We should make the most of every minute we have here. Some people focus on the negative and hold on to the stagnant parts of their lives. To what end? Is "going through the motions" really worth it? At the end of your life, do you want to be known as the kind of person who put their heart and soul into everything and really enjoyed life, or do you want to be known as the kind of person who just got by?

Don't take anything in life for granted, especially your partner. Love is the most powerful force in the universe, and it has bonded the two of you together. Your partner could be gone tomorrow. Or you could be gone. If you've never thought about that before, do it now. If someone told you that one of you would die within a week, how would you change your behavior? Take a while to think seriously about that.

Now that you have come up with the answer about what you would change, the next question is why aren't you doing that now? If you would act differently if you knew death was imminent, then why put it off? Live that way now.

Let Your Spirit Lead

Most of us have felt lost at one time or another in our lives. Whether it is regarding a career path, life purpose, or relationship, we have all felt that we have been tossed from "our path" at some point. If you feel like your relationship path is filled with strife, you need to make some decisions.

As is life, relationships are what you make of them. If you've ever had times when you have felt a true thrill or had a chill run up your back, you need to focus on those things. When your soul speaks to you, it feels good. The key is to find that feeling and follow the drive. It will bring you the aliveness that all humans crave.

You can find the right path by letting your spirit lead. Another way to put it is to follow your intuition. Unfortunately, because intuition makes no logical sense, some people ignore it. Your life usually turns out better when you do listen to "that little voice in your head." If you learn to trust your instincts, you can go on to heights you thought you could never achieve.

Sometimes what we see as "bad" situations only end up leading us to better paths. We might not be able to see it at the time, but the Universe usually has a wonderful road waiting for us, should we choose to take it. Everything happens for reason, and the outcome depends on your ability to make the best of it.

Following your spirit may mean using all of the advice in this book to repair your relationship. If so, put your heart and soul into it; it might mean following a different path with someone new. Either way, let your spirit lead you to a more loving, more exciting relationship that will enrich your life and make you a better person.

Use Mind Programming

Mind programming is simply the process of using your intention to get your subconscious to accept new beliefs. Hypnosis is a powerful tool to accelerate this process, especially in relationships.

Many people are fearful of hypnosis because they perceive it as "giving up control" to the hypnotist. Hypnosis is anything but that.

Biologically speaking, hypnosis is merely the slowing down of brain waves. If you're wide awake and fully alert, you are functioning in a "Beta" brain-wave level. The next level of brain-wave activity is "Alpha." This occurs when you are crossing over into sleep, awakening in the morning, during light hypnosis, or light meditation. "Theta" levels occur in the early stages of sleep, deep hypnosis, or deep meditation. Finally, the "Delta" level is when we are in deep sleep. We all go through this process at least two times a day—when we wake up and when we go to sleep.

Hypnosis/mind programming is ideal to manifest personal change such as building self-confidence, changing habits, losing weight, to stop smoking, improve memory, end behavior problems in children, and eliminate anxiety, fears, and phobias. Some of this hypnotherapy involves past-life regression to uncover the root cause of a problem. At any rate, hypnosis has proven to be an effective tool to improve your life.

We have CDs available that will help you with this process, or you can create your own.

Controlling Outcomes

When you live with expectations and desires, it follows that you want to control outcomes. You want things to unfold in your favor. But you can't control outcomes in life. The best you can hope to do is increase the odds through wisdom.

If you desire a particular outcome, step back and ask yourself, "What's the fear associated with the outcome?"

Explore the fear, including the worst that might happen if things did not turn out in your favor. If you're committed to an outcome, the fear will be related to loss—the loss of love, loss of control, loss of finances, or the loss of self-esteem. Which applies to your situation?

Then ask yourself, "What if I could take the fear out of my desire?"

If there were no fear, the outcome would not matter. Logical.

We're back to resolving fear, a subject we write about a lot, because we are working on it all the time ourselves.

We believe we can create our own reality. We know this to be true when it comes to finding happiness, fulfillment, and living an abundant life. Reality is created by the way we view and accept what is. Don't confuse this with controlling outcomes that affect other people.

In other words, if you want a particular person to love you, that is not within your power to control. The same is true with winning the pageant, getting your book accepted by a major publisher, or desiring a beautiful sunset.

Expectations and the desire to control do not work. Both are fear-based emotions, which we incarnated to rise above.

Some people try to control their thoughts, but this can't be done. You can catch yourself when you're thinking negative. You can use thought-stopping techniques which condition you, over time, to reduce fearful thinking. But out-and-out control of your thoughts isn't an option. What you can control is your behavior and your actions.

A Path With A Heart

"If you want to make God laugh, tell him your future plans," said Woody Allen.

Maybe you're clear on your intent. You know where you want your relationship to go and have mapped a practical path from here to there. But as you make your way down the path, it branches off to the left and there's another branch to the right, and the main path is becoming difficult to traverse.

You decide to exit and follow the natural energy. Now, you're on a new path and you need to reexamine your goal. This path may be leading you in the general direction you want to go, but it's not exactly the destination you envisioned.

Think of taking your journey through life upon the back of an elephant. Life will be a lot easier if you make it all right with yourself to go where the elephant wants to go.

The elephant is destiny.

We make a mistake when we try to force destiny upon the path we "expected" to journey.

Destiny may take the form of an incident, accident, opportunity, or a new person who enters your life . . . and all of a sudden you find yourself exiting onto a new path. The new path is easier, and you now make good time as life unfolds without complications.

When a path is easy, most growth-oriented people lean into the experience, feeling they're going in the right direction. They sense their energy flowing naturally, but when life gets complicated, and you have to force things, your energy jams up — it may be time to consider another path.

Relating this back to you, what path is your soul calling you to walk? A true calling points you in a dharma direction that will unfold easily and naturally. It will be a path with a heart.

Swimming In Circles

We recently read about a woman who needed to clean out her fish bowl but could not find a container in which to place her two goldfish. So, she filled up her bathtub with a couple inches of water and placed the fish in the tub. After cleaning the bowl and returning for the goldfish, she found them swimming in a corner of the tub in a circle no bigger than the fish bowl.

Compare yourself to the fish in the tub. Do your fears, habits, and the patterns of your life keep you swimming in a small circle?

Or do you live dangerously, exploring the potentials of your existence?

Margaret Stortz says, "It takes a lot of courage to release the familiar and seemingly secure, to embrace the new. But there is no real security in what is no longer meaningful. There is more security in the adventurous and exciting, for in movement there is life, and in change there is power."

When making a new decision about your life, Osho advises, "Don't choose the convenient, the comfortable, the respectable, the socially acceptable, the honorable. Choose something that rings a bell in your heart. Choose something that you would like to do in spite of any consequences."

Dangerous ideas? For sure. You could screw up big time. Or, you could find yourself walking down a new path of aliveness.

If you're swimming in small circles, and life isn't as fulfilling as you want it to be, consider your level of aliveness. Aliveness is excitement, enjoyment in doing what you do. It's that blood-pumping exhilaration, challenge, joy, stimulation, and pleasure that makes life worth living.

If you've traded freedom and aliveness for security, there is no time like the present to consider adding some joyous new challenges to your life.

Behavior vs. Feelings

A sensible individual does not waste time and energy trying to directly control their feelings, because feelings cannot be manipulated by the will. "We cannot make ourselves feel confident or satisfied or grateful or loving or courageous just by concentrating or wishing we were so. Try it. It doesn't work with any consistency at all," says David K. Reynolds Ph.D. in *Even in summer the ice doesn't melt.*

You can will yourself to go to work or spend an evening with someone you don't like, or walk the dog, even when you do not feel like it. To be mature is to be responsible for your actions, regardless of your feelings. But, you cannot control what you feel. If you do not like what you are feeling, accept the feeling, without resistance, and simply go on about your life. In time, the feeling will pass, other feelings will arise. The intensity of a feeling does not last forever.

We often quote a Reynolds line, "Behavior wags the tail of feelings." In other words, you can control your behavior, which in time may alter how you feel in a particular life area. If you watch pornography (behavior), you're going to generate sex-related emotions (feelings). If you avoid helping someone you care about (behavior), you're going to lower self-esteem (feelings). If your boyfriend left because you demanded he do what you wanted him to do (behavior), you now feel depressed about being alone (feelings).

You can control your behavior no matter how turbulent your emotional life. When you do, your feelings tend to settle down relatively quickly. When you allow yourself to express wild extremes of behavior in response to extreme feelings, you perpetuate the intense emotions.

Accept your feelings, knowing they will fade over time unless you do something to restimulate them. You are not responsible for what you feel, but you are responsible for what you do no matter what you are feeling.

Love Yourself

The key to a successful and happy relationship is to be comfortable and peaceful with who you are. It is not possible to be truly joyous unless you feel good about yourself. The quality of your relationship and how your partner treats you stems from this simple truth.

Unfortunately, many people do not love themselves. They don't realize the importance of loving yourself first before you can truly, deeply love another person. Or, they don't believe it can be done. Even if they think it can, the effort required seems like an insurmountable feat. Disbelief and unwillingness to change are the most common responses.

Self-love is actually the source of receiving what you want. Not just in relationships, but in life. It is so important to be in touch with the attitudes you have about yourself because they come through in your actions to others. Your attitudes can exist as thoughts, behaviors, and what you say. If none of these are positive, then you are sabotaging your inner sense of well-being, and, thus, your relationship.

Your level of self-love is not constant. For example, perhaps when you got married, you were a slim 120 pounds. However, 10 years and three children later, you have inched up to 170 pounds. As a result, you hate how you look, and it shows in the way you interact with others. You might act uninterested in sex because you are embarrassed by your body, and your partner might interpret what is really self-hatred as a personal rejection to him. This obviously causes many relationship problems.

All your happiness, including your level of satisfaction with your relationship, is filtered through how you view yourself. If you want positive changes in your relationship, then there is something you must change in yourself first. Try to discover what that is, work on it, and then see the positive effects it has on your partner.

Affirmations

An affirmation is a statement of intention. It is a mental note that is sent to the Universe about something you want. As a tool, it is relatively simple: repeat an optimistic desire with the intention of creating it. This will allow it to become your truth. With continued use, affirmations have incredible power for manifesting what you desire.

They also focus your mind. Once you have a clear goal, you can create several affirmations to support the creation of your desire. If you don't focus your mind on what you want, it will go off in a thousand different directions. What you pay attention to, you create. If you don't pay attention to positive affirmations about your relationship, then they cannot possibly come into being.

Now is the time to direct your mind. Make it go in the direction you want it to go. Don't allow it to wander off into a ditch, or that is exactly where you will find your relationship. Although negative programming certainly exists within your brain, affirmations can build other patterns of neural pathways.

Make your affirmations as positive as you can. For example, instead of saying "John will no longer be unloving and messy," it is important to say, "John is now loving and cleans the house voluntarily." As you can see, it says the same thing, but the latter is much more positive. If you use the first affirmation, your mind will focus on the word "unloving." The subconscious mind does not understand negatives, so phrase your affirmations as if they already exist and in the most positive terms.

Whether you realize it or not, you have made many negative conclusions about yourself and your relationship. Affirmations can help you greatly. Don't forget to repeat them as often as possible for maximum results (at least 5 to 10 times a day) until you feel your mood begin to change.

The Spiritual Connection

A true spiritual connection is when two people have compatibility on four levels: emotional, intellectual, physical, and spiritual. Few couples have a perfect connection on all levels. Usually they work well on a one or two but never reach all four. It takes a special pairing to form a spiritual union like this.

Let's discuss the four levels individually. How do you connect with your partner on an emotional level? When we say "emotional," we don't necessarily mean someone who cries at the drop of a hat. Rather, we mean their ability to plug into another person's emotions. Do they care, respond, nurture?

Intellectually, some people are out of balance. One partner may enjoy reading and exploring philosophical topics while the other is content to watch television and play video games. While there is nothing inherently wrong with these activities, it creates a disconnect between the people.

On a physical level, both partners must agree on the frequency and quality of their sex life. If the two people are out of sync, it can affect the overall quality of their relationship. Even though much of sexual desire is a personal preference, a rhythm can be established through communicating and acting on each person's desires.

Spiritual sameness is also a necessary element. This does not mean that you have to be the same religion. If spirituality or religion is important to you and an integral part of your life, it helps if you and your partner see "eye to eye." Even if there is mere tolerance of the others' spiritual beliefs, that is not enough because there is not true sharing.

If your relationship doesn't possess all four elements of a spiritual connection, take some time to assess whether it's worth repairing. Or, maybe, you should move on to someone else who can complete you in a more effective manner.

Invoke the Law of Desire

We discuss several Universal Laws in this book. If you learn how to use them in a positive manner, they will all work together to make your life better. One law that is vitally important to relationship improvement is the Law of Desire.

In order to harness its power, you must first be clear on your goal. Many people wish their relationship was better, but as those words come past their lips, subconsciously, they know that more would be required of them if, in fact, it were to happen. As a result, most people don't accomplish what they set out to do because they are not clear on their desire.

If you have defined your relationship goals and are clear on your destination, you can put the Law of Desire to work for you, as long as your intentions are based in love and not fear.

The first step is repeat positive affirmations to let the Universe know your desire. Next, you open up to let your hopes become your beliefs. Don't just hope your relationship will get better. Believe it. Failure is not an option. That is the attitude you must have in order to manifest a better relationship.

You have to believe you are worthy of having the kind of relationship you desire. For example, perhaps, you constantly complain that your partner is lazy about working on your partnership. If he were to suddenly step up to the plate and require more of you, do you think you are worthy of receiving the unconditional love you think you desire? You may find that deep down in your belief system, you don't. If that is the case, it could be standing in the way of your desire.

Let your positive hopes become your beliefs. Then focus energy on your desires. Visualize them coming true. Feel it. Believe it. And it will be yours.

Grieve

Nobody likes to grieve because that means that we have something in our life for which we feel sorrow. In fact, grief is probably one of the most difficult things in life to deal with. Unfortunately, relationships are a great source of grief, but many people ignore these feelings instead of dealing with them.

It seems logical that most relationship grieving would occur after it is over. However, it is important to grieve even when you are in the relationship. Most people simply intellectualize their frustrations instead of dealing with their emotions.

Perhaps, you are in a relationship where the person you are with has changed considerably and as much as you've tried to hold things together, the person you fell in love with is "gone." Yes, they are there physically, but intellectually and emotionally, they are like a different person. In a situation like this, it is important not to ignore your feelings of grief but rather deal with them on an ongoing basis.

The loss of anything in a relationship can be overwhelming, but not allowing yourself to grieve can be a big mistake. It makes your energy heavier and denser, and then pretty soon you'll be broadcasting depressing vibrations, and when you send out negative vibes to the Universe, you will get nothing but negative circumstances back. This could be in the form of relationship problems or anything else.

Here are the steps to follow: **1|** acknowledge your sorrow, **2|** allow yourself to fully express your sadness and negative emotions for as long as you need to, and **3|** when you are finished expressing the grief, then release it. Only by feeling the grief will you be able to set yourself free. Instead of looking at grieving as a negative experience, re-frame it and consider it a cleansing process. It helps you turn your pain into knowledge, power, and eventually, happiness.

Depression

Because of its frequency, depression is called "the common cold of psychiatry." Depression affects millions, and at least one third of the population will experience it sometime in their lives. This is a devastating disease that makes people feel hopeless and isolated. It can be terribly damaging to a relationship. The good news, though, is most depressed people fully recover.

The key symptoms of depression are a low pessimistic mood or a loss of interest in things that were previously fulfilling and enjoyable. Another indicator might be the inability to concentrate, often accompanied by a lack of energy. Minor tasks become a huge effort. Sleep patterns may change, and there can be a loss of appetite. Self-confidence can take a dip, and some people will become indecisive and/or develop deep feelings of guilt and begin blaming themselves for their past inadequacies.

Each case of depression is different, but they are usually categorized as mild, moderate, or severe. In cases of mild depression, some of the above mentioned symptoms will be present, but the individual can still function normally. With severe depression, all the symptoms will be present to the degree the individual will probably be unable to work or care for their children. They will no longer be interested in social activities or in maintaining relationships with others.

Other forms include mania and bipolar depression, post-natal depression, and seasonal affective disorder that strikes people during the long, dark, cold-winter months.

Trying to find what causes depression can be a big order and likely involves a complicated mix of biological, social, and psychological factors. Although we know changes in brain chemistry occur during depression, it is not known what triggers the changes. Stress and depression are closely related, and people are more likely to become depressed in the weeks and months following a stressful event such as the death of someone close, divorce, a job loss, financial difficulties, or marital discord.

Doctors and counselors have interview formulas to detect depression, which can be treated with medication and/or talk therapy for starters. There are also complementary therapies that have been proven to help, such as acupuncture, aromatherapy, massage, music therapy, and relaxation. Exercise is highly recommended, especially disciplines such as yoga. If you think you or your partner is depressed, get help.

"Why?"

As we move from infatuation into a long-term partnership, often the quality of the relationship declines. At first, our partner is perfect in our eyes. Then, as time goes on, that person loses his or her "star quality." At this point, most people find themselves asking "why?" Why did the relationship deteriorate? Why?

The reason "why" things happened the way they did is sometimes unknowable. In fact, there is usually no one reason. Perhaps, you're the kind of person who thinks that "if only we could communicate better, then we would be happier." Or, perhaps, you blame your circumstances on the fact that your mate works too much. The list could go on and on.

If you keep asking "why," try to figure out if you are really just trying to place blame on your partner. People who do this are playing the "victim" role. You are not at the complete mercy of outside circumstances (including the actions of your partner). You have to claim your power and realize that life is what you make if it, including your relationship.

While it is more common for people to blame their partners, some people blame themselves instead. They have thoughts such as, "I'm not attractive enough," "If only I lost weight," "I'm too demanding," or "I'm not doing enough for my mate."

It is not healthy to blame anyone or anything. Instead, try to get out of the mindset of blame. You are not totally to blame and neither is your partner. You both share the responsibility.

The reasons "why" come in many forms. Here are just a few common factors that do tend to cause relationship problems:

- Poor communication
- Poor self-image(s)

- Unawareness of needs and desires
- Past events that contribute to mental states
- Psychological issues

Change what you can. As for the rest of it, accept "what is" and move on.

Desirelessness

In order to have growth, you must "desire." This is true in any area of your life. For example, if you don't desire a new car, you won't get one. If you don't desire a better job, you won't pursue new opportunities. By the same token, if you don't desire something better in your relationship, then how can you possibly get it? If you don't "desire," you can't create anything new.

You may be at a point of desirelessness in your relationship. If your mate came to you tomorrow and said, "What do you want me to do or to change? I'll do anything to make you happy!" What would you say? Would you gladly pull out a long list of things for him/her to change? Or would you simply say, "You're too late." If your answer would be the latter, there was probably a time when you needed many things that you didn't get, and, somewhere along the road, you lost the desire for change and just settled into complacency.

In many areas of life, it's important to accept "what is" and not stress about the things you can't change. However, if this mental attitude had led you to a stagnant relationship, then that is not an acceptable option. Why are you tolerating it?

You have two choices. First, try to find desire. You may be asking, "How do I do that?" Unfortunately, we don't have those answers for you. It's different for everyone. But, if you put in the effort to find the desire, but can't, then you only have one more choice: let go.

Ultimately, it comes down to asking yourself what kind of life you want to lead: one filled with growth or one filled with stagnancy? Yes, it is difficult to say good-bye to your mate, but isn't that better than living the rest of your life with the constant "blahs?"

Join an Online Dating Service

One way to generate aliveness in your life as you move on from your relationship is to join an online dating service or some other internet community where you can communicate with people of the opposite sex. This tip is especially useful for single parents and/or if you work in a place where there are not many dating options. The "stigma" of internet dating is lifting, and, thus, it is becoming the "in" thing to do.

However, some people are fearful of "getting back out there" in the dating world. If *you* are, you do not actually have to go on dates with these people or even meet face-to-face. What it does mean is that you are generating some "fire in your soul." Typically, when we see that others find us attractive (whether that is either physical or personality-based), we have a renewed sense of self-worth. We begin to remember what is great about us and why we are worthy of a quality partner.

By generating excitement, aliveness, and feelings of self-worth, you will not only have some fun, but you will also start projecting positive thoughts and emotions. These thoughts and emotions emanate from you and will draw in more positive experiences. The energy that you send out to other people will be positive. Then maybe "Mr./Ms. Right" will then pick up on your good vibrations at a subconscious level.

Unless you have a huge circle of friends, no kids, and really enjoy the bar scene, this is a great option. It provides you the opportunity to "weed out" a lot of people before you even go on your first date. Even if you don't like the person, you know there are a lot more people waiting to take you out.

This option can generate some incredible energy that may circle back to your whole life and create more new experiences for you.

Follow Your Intuition, Not Your Logic

We are taught to rely on our logic. Supposedly, it is the most reliable guide you can have throughout your life. Most people think they can make the best decisions by having all the "facts" and then coming to a rational conclusion. However, this approach isn't always the best.

We are encouraged to ignore our intuition. In fact, most people probably wouldn't even recognize their intuition in action if it were to slap them upside the head. It's one of those great mysteries of life that no one can define. But it's always there. Take some time to tune into it. Let us give you an example.

Let's say you just had a string of bad dates. Then, all of a sudden, your friend sets you up with someone, and the minute you meet him, you think "YOWSA!! I LOVE THIS PERSON!!" He is fun, friendly, interesting, attractive, and pretty much almost everything you were missing in the previous ten dates. But, on your second date, he cancels at the last minute as your babysitter is walking through the door. You are expecting a good excuse, like he is in the emergency room. You don't get one. Instead, all you get is, "Gosh, I'm so sorry, but all this crap just hit me, and I can't make it tonight." It doesn't matter that your babysitter is there, and you are dressed to the nines and ready for a night out on the town. He cancels for no good reason.

What do you do? If you follow your logic, you say "I like him so much, and I'm sure he'll never do it again." Or do you follow your intuition that says, "Dump the guy. If he does this to you on the second date, how reliable can the man be?" This is not to say you can't give him a few more dates, but chances are your intuition is always right.

Don't Compromise This Time

Life is full of compromises, especially in relationships. When we say "don't compromise" we mean, "don't settle for anything less than what you want." Maybe having a man who is a good listener is very important to you. Then, you meet a guy who, in many other ways, meets the criteria as your "perfect guy," but he is the worst listener in the world. What do you do? In most cases, people usually just shrug their shoulders and ignore it because they like the other parts of that person. That could get you into trouble down the road.

If you look back on some of your relationships, you can probably see the "red flags" that you chose to ignore. Somewhere in the back of your mind, your intuition screamed "THIS IS GOING TO BE A PROBLEM." But lots of times people's logic contradicts: "Aww, who cares? It's not that big of a deal. It's better than starting all over and trying to find someone new. Nobody's perfect."

Some other examples of compromising: **1|** You want a fun guy who gives you a giddy, exciting feeling in your stomach every time you think about him. You meet a guy who you find attractive, has a great sense of humor, and is perfect in every other way, but you don't get giddy over him. Is that a "red flag?" Probably. If you choose to continue, you will probably be compromising and **2|** You want a successful partner...someone who makes at least as much money per year as you do, if not more. Then you meet this wonderful man who makes significantly less than you would like. You talk yourself into thinking you are a "gold digger" and that "money isn't everything." But, sometimes someone's bank account has a direct relation to their goals, dreams, or ability to dedicate themselves to something.

Remember, your intuition is the most reliable guidance you get. ***Follow it.***

Don't Be Desperate

We have known people who think it's better to be with "anyone" than be alone. Are you one of those people? Or, perhaps, you're the kind of person who cannot break up with someone unless you have another person lined up to take his/her place. Are you one of ***those*** people? If you answered yes, you might be too desperate.

Desperation is a negative emotion. Any fear-based emotion such as jealousy, possessiveness, anxiety, or anger can affect your whole life. It has been proven that different emotions can be photographed and their rate of vibration can be measured. The negative emotions like desperation are very slow-vibrating. But emotions such as joy, love, or appreciation vibrate very quickly. Scientists have found that the slow emotions attract more negative conditions in one's life.

If you are the kind of person who "needs a man" or "needs a woman," get out of the mindset. You might be repelling the very thing you want most in your life. If nothing else, anyone can spot a desperate person a mile away, and most don't want to be around them. Yes, it is nice to have someone want you, but to have someone keep you around only because they ***need someone—anyone***—in their lives … well, that is not how most people want to exist in relationships.

Admitting you are desperate can be difficult at best. No one wants to admit they are desperate. Take some time to be honest with yourself. Once you discover your level of desperation, you can start to change it.

Being alone can be a wonderful experience. It can lead to intense learning. It forces you to look at you and only ***you.*** By spending some time with yourself, you will hopefully not only get to know yourself better, you will also get to like yourself better. This will definitely help you attract your perfect mate.

Be Patient

Sometimes the Universe takes its own sweet time. In fact, it seems like we are usually at the mercy of its timeline and not our own. I'm sure you know what we are talking about, because it happens to all of us.

For example, sometimes we are all taken on a twisting and turning journey in life not knowing where it will lead. You "see" your destination. You can feel it and taste it. You know where you want to end up. Why do you often ask yourself, "How the heck did I end up ***here?***" Usually, "ending up ***here***" is merely a step towards your destination. You don't know it at the time, but if you didn't go through these unexpected experiences, then you may not arrive where you want to be.

Perhaps, you wanted a well-paying satisfying job at an advertising agency when you graduated from college, but all you found was a lousy $12,000-a-year job doing nothing but twiddling your thumbs. You think "***How did I end up here?***" You think the Universe obviously misunderstood your request and focused you in the wrong direction. Right? Wrong. Perhaps you needed to wait a while so you could meet the perfect person who would steer you on a completely different career path. You were just in a holding pattern, you just didn't know it.

You will find this in your romantic life as well. ***Why did this relationship have to end? Why am I only finding dorks to date? Why have I found this great guy, but I don't feel like he's "the one?"*** Have faith. The Universe knows what it's doing. If you have the attitude of "everything happens for a reason" and "everything leads to the highest good of all," then you can't go wrong. Get in the passenger's seat, be patient, and enjoy the ride. Even the bumpy parts.

Negotiate Boundaries

Everyone has boundaries, but many of us have not taken the time to think about what they are. First, how do we define the word "boundary?" A boundary is a "comfort zone" or a "requirement" for you to feel like ***you***. Some of us have very narrow boundaries, and others' are quite broad.

For example, maybe you are an "anything goes" kind of person. You are spontaneous, don't plan a lot, will try anything new, and share everything with anyone. Then, you meet someone who you fall head-over-heels for. This person, at least on the surface, is everything you ever wanted: great personality, good looks, well-educated, and interesting. Your attitude is, "what could possible go wrong?" The answer is: a lot. When we are in a relationship with someone, our boundaries meet their boundaries, and sometimes they clash. This is one of the many things that can get relationships into trouble.

People have endless kinds of boundaries: sexual, adventurous, or self-disclosure, just to name a few. But let's take a strange example to further illustrate our point. Say that perfect person you just met doesn't like sharing their food with anyone. And, because you have broad boundaries, you love doing it. In your mind, sharing everything with your significant other is a sign of love, but apparently is not true for your new partner. It makes them anxious. Unless you come to understand and respect this, something as silly as food-sharing could eventually become a major point of contention in the relationship.

In order to understand how to get along with someone who has different boundaries, you must first know your own. Then, ask the other person about theirs, and respect them … even if you don't understand them. Chances are, if they are not *your* boundaries, then you *won't* understand them, but that doesn't mean that they are not important to your new partner. It is important remember that.

Write Down Your Future Partner's Qualities

Many people complain that they can't find "the one" or their mantra is "all the good ones are taken." Those statements imply that you will know "the one" or at least a "good one" when they walk up to you. That may not always be the case.

Most people have not written down the qualities of their perfect partner. Instead, they just wander aimlessly through life and hope to find someone that likes them. Does that mean that they are "the one?" Not necessarily. You will not be able to find "the one" until you have first defined for yourself—and for the Universe—what that means.

Go ahead and take out a piece of paper right now and do this exercise. Answer the following questions: What does he/she look like? Be sure to include specifics like: height, weight, eye color, hair (color/bald/full head of hair/length), body type, facial features. What age range (example: aged 30–45)? What income level? What education level? Job type? Marital status?

Personality characteristics? This is a particularly important one, and you should be specific. For example, you might include qualities such as fun, outgoing, friendly, easy-going, humorous, optimist, romantic, nurturing, affectionate, good communicator, passionate, intelligent, ambitious, mature, patient, level-headed, self-aware, non-judgmental, balanced, self-assured, empathetic, honest, trustworthy, or humble.

Other things to consider: Likes kids? Sexual appetite? Likes traveling? Outlook on life? Religious/spiritual beliefs? How he/she treats others? Lifestyle? Drinker or non-drinker? Active/passive?

These are merely some examples to start you on your quest to find "the one." The qualities you might want, someone else might not want. Everyone will answer these differently. Don't forget to add ideas of your own.

Once you are done with this activity, put the list into an envelope. Then take time every day to meditate and think about that perfect person and have faith that the Universe will bring him or her to you.

Beware of "Good Interviewers"

When you go on a job interview, what do you wear? Sweatpants? No, of course not. Presumably (and depending on the type of job for which you are interviewing), you will dress up in a suit. How do you act? Do you crack rude jokes and act like you don't care? No, of course not. When people are interviewing for a job, they put on their best performance. They have to, because if they don't, then they won't get the job.

Let's be honest: dating is the same as a job interview. Each person is dressing up and looking their best. They are also putting on their best personality so the other will be enchanted with them. In other words, many of us do not present our true self early on in the dating process.

Just like with job interviews, some people are great at becoming someone they are not to get the job. Others are more their true selves. However, to some degree, we are all "on stage." The person who captivates you on the first three dates may turn into someone who — three months or three years later — is ignoring your needs in favor of his/her own.

It's important to realize we are all "interviewers." Some people you "hire" will work out great, and you will be happy with their performance. With others, you will say, "What the heck was I thinking??" The problem is, you probably weren't thinking. You were too wrapped up in their charisma to acknowledge the fact that what you see now is not what you are going to be seeing later.

Some people's true selves will emerge very soon. Others may take years. But nevertheless, a person cannot hide who they really are forever. Eventually, they will be themselves around you 24/7. So make sure ***that*** self is the one you want to date. Not the "good interviewer."

"Dater" or "Relationship Person"?

There are two kinds of people in the world: "daters" and "relationship" people. The two of us happen to both be "relationship people." We love to have the companionship of someone We think the whole point to the dating game is to ultimately fall deeply in love and then spend the rest of your life with one person.

Here's a news-flash for "relationship" people: ***not everyone wants a relationship.*** Some people actually prefer casually dating over a long term commitment. As much as you might not understand it, it's true. ***Not everyone likes being in a relationship.***

This, of course, presents problems when you are dating. Perhaps, you meet someone who sweeps you off your feet on the first date. That night, you lay in bed convinced you have just met "The One" and are already planning your life together. Meanwhile, Mr./Ms. Wonderful might be just thinking how great it is to meet someone fun that they can date twice a month or whenever ***they*** feel like it. Obviously, this does not add up to the perfect relationship for ***you***.

There are many reasons someone might be a "dater." The first thing that comes to mind is fear of emotional intimacy. Sexual intimacy may not be a problem. Sometimes daters are also the "sleep-around" type. For anyone who has ever seen an episode of *Sex and the City*, the character that epitomizes this is Samantha. She was almost "relationship-phobic," but she loved to have sex. This character is fictionalized and exaggerated, but she is the extreme version of a "dater."

If you find yourself being the only one trying to maintain contact with that person who just swept you off your feet, well, either that person doesn't like you very much, or perhaps—just perhaps—that person is a "dater." If you want a quality relationship, it is best to move on.

Know What You Want Right Now

If you are just coming off a long term marriage or relationship, you need to think about what you want to do ***right now.*** Do you just want to be alone for a while? Do you want to casually date? Do you want to find another serious relationship or marriage?

Being alone for a while is a good option for some. It can lead to self-discovery and introspection. That is a great way to heal and figure out what you want next time around. Rushing into a new relationships isn't always the best answer.

Or, say you want to get out there and date again. Then think about ***why*** you are dating ***right now***. What do you want? What are you ready for? What you ***think*** you want and are ready for might be completely different than what you ***really*** want and are ready for.

There are many people who won't date someone who has recently broken off a long term relationship or marriage. That may be a good rule. Research shows that it takes around two years for a person to really get over, heal, and move on from a previous serious relationship

If you decide to date, what is your goal? Casual dating? Serious relationship? Marriage? Or, you simply want to make new friends. Maybe you and your ex-partner didn't have any single friends, and now, all of a sudden, you realize that all your friends have family commitments and cannot live the single life like you. Then what? Maybe dating would be a good option for you. You will meet different people and get to know other singles, even if you don't make a romantic connection. The tricky part of this strategy is being honest about your goals, whatever they are. Be sure to tell your dates what you want. That way, they will know what they are getting into.

Go With The Flow

In the world of dating, it's easy to get caught up in all the drama. After all, if you're like most people, you prefer being in a committed relationship (although not all people prefer this). Chances are, at some point in the dating process you will probably find yourself questioning why certain things are or are not happening. Where is "The One" you've always dreamed of?

Let's say you've joined an online dating service. The nature of this type of dating can be fun yet confusing. There are many single people who are "thrown together" on a website all looking to connect with someone. You might find yourself chatting with this really great person for a while. You get your hopes up; could they be "the one?" You may even go out on a date with them and think you really hit it off. Then…POOF! They're gone. No more response. You torture yourself thinking, "Was it something I said?" or "Am I not good looking enough? Not witty enough in my emails? What went wrong?"

Our advice to you is to stop analyzing it and move on. Don't think it's something you did or didn't do. Do not think you are inadequate in any way. That is not true. You are a real catch who deserves being treated like royalty.

Instead, realize that there is a natural flow to the Universe. The Universe has a plan. If you've had 5 dates canceled on you in rapid succession, know that there is a ***reason***. There may be lessons for you to learn. Perhaps, the Universe doesn't want you involved with anyone when "The One" becomes available. Remember, everything happens at the perfect time in the perfect way. If you have this attitude, you will enjoy every step of your dating journey.

Don't Forget to Pause

When a relationship ends, many of us quickly look ahead to see who might come along next in our lives. Our society conditions us to think that being a part of a couple is normal, and if you find yourself single, you must quickly change that.

Now might be the time to pause and reflect on your past relationship, your life, and what might come to you in the future. Wait patiently, because the Universe is shifting and re-arranging your life. You might be able to see some of what is happening, but more often than not, you won't.

Your life is changing, and there might be little you can control at this time. That is okay. Don't waste your energy attempting to swim upstream and don't respond to your fear-based emotions. If you do, you just end up resisting "what is." The end result could be worse; you could draw a more undesirable situation into your life and perpetuate its influence in your life.

The situation you are in may last days, weeks, months, or even years but rest assured that light will appear at the end of the tunnel. Life ***will*** get better. It is best to have the attitude of "everything happens for a reason" and "things can only go up from here." If you believe it, then it's true.

Instead of trying to force your romantic life to take on the direction ***you*** want it to, why not sit back and reflect on what you've done so far. How can you be a better romantic partner in the future? What can you do to make yourself whole? How can you grow as a person so when you do meet that perfect someone, you will be ready? What does your ideal romantic relationship look like? Take some time to review your past and learn from it. It will pay off in the long run.

Don't Care About What Other People Think

Our society sets up unwritten rules and expectations for people to follow. In many ways, it expects us to follow a uniform way of living and behaving, and anyone who is outside the norm is an outcast. As a result, people wear the masks of the proper clothing, manners, and etiquette. People wander through life being so caught up in society's expectations that they sometimes lose their own identity.

When this reality is applied to relationships, you can see it in many areas. For example, there are parents who pressure their sons or daughters to get married. This implies that someone is not whole unless they have a romantic partner. This, of course, is untrue. To make things worse, there is the unspoken pressure of society on women to be married by a certain age, or they might end up as an "old maid." Once someone does get married, then comes the inevitable question of when the couple will have children. Again, this implies that someone cannot be whole or happy without offspring.

You might be facing this sort of pressure from family, friends, or society at large. If so, take a moment to ponder this question: Do you project who you really are, or are you the person that others want you to be? If you are living as the person that others want you to be, then you are basing these relationships on your willingness to be manipulated. If you don't comply, some form of rejection will be the result.

Take some time to think about how society's norms and other's expectations are shaping your feelings and your behavior. Are they affecting you? And if so, do you need to stop repressing who you really are? If you did, what would be the worst that could happen? What would be the best that could happen?

Embrace Risk

Humans need challenge to grow. We cannot become a better person without facing and overcoming certain challenges. However, most challenges require risk and moving on from your relationship is no different. It will require risk.

Helen Keller said, "Security is mostly a superstition. It does not exist in nature, nor do the children of men as a whole experience it. Avoiding danger is no safer in the long run than outright exposure. Life is either a daring adventure or nothing."

Think about that statement. It is so true. Even though we think we have a secure job, a roof over our head, and food to eat, anything could happen at any moment. A natural disaster could drastically change our way of life in a blink of an eye. A world war could also change how we all live. A wise man once said, "The only thing constant is change." Therefore, what Helen Keller said is true. Security is nothing more than an illusion. Yet, we trick ourselves into thinking that we are secure when we are in a relationship, but we are not.

If security does not exist, why not embrace taking some big risks in your life? Perhaps, you are an introverted person who does not like big social events. You generally shy away from having to have much social interaction on a large scale. Yet, one of your friends invites you to a Super Bowl party at her house. To most people, going to a party does not involve much risk, but to you it does. You never know who you are going to meet. Or, your best friend begs you to come to a speed dating event. You think the idea is dumb. But remember: nothing ventured, nothing gained. You never know who you might meet.

Everyone assesses risks differently, so get ready to take one! Life is short!

Welcome The New Beginning

Unfortunately, our society programs us to be pessimistic. Instead of looking at what is good about a situation, most people naturally gravitate to seeing what is bad. When someone has ended a relationship, rarely do they embrace their new status and say "Oh good! Now I get to start all over!" Instead, they are more likely to say, "Where do I go from here?" That uncertainty is not a welcome feeling to most people.

New beginnings always require stepping into the unknown. That's why they are scary. Your life right now might be filled with confusion or even chaos. You probably wish that your fairy godparent would come down and show you the way to a brand-new romantic partner.

New beginnings are an ideal time to move from an attached mind to a detached one. The vast majority of people live their lives only knowing an attached mind. An attached mind is one that fluctuates from positive to negative as outside conditions change. A detached mind only fluctuates from positive to neutral as outside conditions change. You accept all the joy and happiness that life had to offer, but your state of mind never drops farther than neutral because you understand that you can't control unalterable realities.

Try to find a way to enjoy and appreciate the opportunity to start over. Your relationship was probably not bringing you much joy or else it would not be over. Instead of wallowing in the sadness of what just ended, rejoice in the happiness of what might begin. The saying "God never closes a door where he doesn't open a window" is very true. Don't dwell on the negative; appreciate the opportunity to develop detached mind and move forward with the enthusiasm of an excited child.

Don't Worry About Your Age

Oftentimes when someone finds him or herself single at an older age, they begin to panic and think that no one will want to date someone their age. Unfortunately, our society is "youth-based." In other words, collectively, we value looking and acting young. At some point, you might wonder how you will fit in with this societal mindset.

It is important to know that there is much more to youth than just your age. You need to be aware that joy and harmony are youthful energies, while negativity and disharmony are old ones. If you always seek the positive side of any situation and remain joyful, you will also remain youthful. Even though your body will keep aging with natural law, your mind and spirit can remain forever young.

When you project youthful energy, you are also adventurous and experience aliveness and excitement in whatever you do. Only someone youthful will take the risks that make life worth living. If you allow yourself to become old in spirit, you begin to fear losing. When you do that, you start to trade growth opportunities and challenges for security and comfort.

Joy is not generated by people and things outside yourself. The feeling of joy that comes and goes with the change of outside conditions does not last. True joy — and, thus, youthfulness — comes from deep within.

No matter your age, if you project youthful energy into the world, it is inevitable that others will be drawn to you. Everyone likes to be around (and date) people who are happy and joyous. If all you dwell on is your age and think "who would want me?" — you will be projecting that energy to others. They will pick up on it and want to stay away from you. Forget about your age as a number and focus on your attitude and energy. You will likely find a great match.

Seek Awareness of Your Truth

Sometimes people don't even know who they are if they are not in a relationship. Many people attach their identity on their partner and/or their relationship status. If you find yourself single and confused, this may be the perfect time to discover who you are and that includes finding your own truth.

Many of your truths are buried in the memory banks of your subconscious mind. The subconscious contains knowledge, understanding, talents, abilities, and memories of those past events that make you feel guilty or fearful. Since you do not consciously know about them, you lack the awareness to rise above them. However, this does not mean that they are not affecting you. You still experience the undesirable hidden programming.

Awareness is measured by how much you let yourself know your own truth. You must explore what restricts and motivates you in relationships. Answers are never difficult if you can ask the right questions.

You may want to start with questions like these: Why do you want a relationship? What kind of person are you? Selfish or selfless? What are you core values? What do you expect out of other people? What do you expect out of yourself? How well do you know yourself?

For example, if you are the kind of person who cannot date anyone outside of your faith, you can't imagine being with anyone who didn't see the world the same way.

Or, you are a very good communicator and like to have frequent conversations about the state of your relationship. If you try to be with a partner who is more the silent type, that will inevitably create problems.

In other words, know who you are and what you stand for—your ***truth.***

Being Single

Problem or Opportunity?

Many people enjoy being in a relationship. Others enjoy being single. If you're not the kind of person who enjoys the single life, it is likely that you have labeled it as a "problem." If you have done this, you might find yourself complaining and worrying and verbalizing your plight over and over.

It is important to know that the more you talk about your "problem" of being single, the more you program that negative reality into your subconscious mind. In the long run, it just complicates your situation even further.

Instead of viewing it as a problem, consider viewing it as an opportunity. Being single is a fantastic opportunity to learn and grow. The only difference between problem-oriented singles and opportunity-oriented singles is ***attitude***. If you view being unattached as an opportunity, then you no longer have a problem!

If you're still struggling with how to see your situation as a growth opportunity, then give this some consideration. Maybe when you were in the relationship that just ended, you didn't socialize very much with other people. Some couples tend to do that, especially if you have children. The demands of childcare are so intense sometimes that it is easy to neglect your social life. Or, people fall into a rut with no new experiences coming their way.

You should appreciate the opportunity to get back out into the social arena and make some new friends. Or, go on some interesting dates and have some new experiences. Perhaps, a new friend of yours will teach you to skydive or hang-glide.

Even if you just look at your single life as the opportunity to find someone who is a much better match for you, then that is a reason to celebrate. Appreciate the fact that you are not stuck in the negative relationship you just ended.

Leave Your Options Open

It is likely that at some point when you are single, you will find someone you really like. The only problem might be that you meet this person in the office or through a friend. While that's wonderful, sometimes that person may not notice you in a romantic way. What do you do? Many people's tendencies are to wait around for the person to "come to their senses" and ask them out on a date. Maybe that will happen, and maybe it won't.

If someone likes you enough, they will want to date you. In fact, it seems like nothing will hold them back if it feels right. If you find yourself in a situation where you are not getting the proper attention from the object of your affection, then let it go.

Sometimes people find themselves in situations where they are just merely having sex with someone. In other words, you might call the relationship "friends with benefits." This is fine for some people. But is it ***really*** fine with you? Do you really want that kind of "relationship" (or lack thereof)? Think about it: maybe your sexual partner has everything they want. You are having sex with them, and they don't have to really date or commit to you in any way. Why would you put up with that (unless, of course, you are that person)?

Don't put all your eggs in one basket. Leave your options open. Don't think "it's better than nothing." That's not good enough for you! If you're waiting around for your friend to ask you out on a real date (whether you are sleeping with them or not), ***don't***. Don't wait around for them. Instead, go find someone who wants the same kind of relationship you do and don't settle for anything less.

Don't Let Charm Blind You

Not everyone has a charismatic personality. When you find someone who does, you could be pulled in by their charm—but don't forget to look beneath the surface to see what else is there.

For example, let's say you have had a string of disappointing dates. All these people were very nice and you had an enjoyable time, but no one stood out and you were not very attracted to any of them. Then—suddenly—the charming one comes along. You know from the moment they hug you that this is going to be a ***good*** date. You have immediate rapport. You feel as if you've known each other forever. You laugh and talk your way through the whole evening. You talk about what a rare connection the two of you have. You both program each other's numbers into your cell phones. It must be destined, right?

Well, maybe not. It was only one date. There are so many things you do ***not*** know about this person, and even the information that you do have may have been misinterpreted by you as representative of their personality.

Let us give you a real-life example. We have a friend who had almost the exact experience as above. One of the things that intrigued her about this guy is that he was once a "Dead Head"—he followed the Grateful Dead around for years. Later he finds out he has a child with someone. So, he gives up his Dead Head life and moves to be near the child so he can help raise her. Upon hearing this story, she thinks he's heroic. However, after finding out more about him, she realized she should have focused upon the fact that he was a ***Dead Head*** for eight years. Unfortunately, once she got to know him, that piece of information was really much more representative of his overall personality.

The moral of the story is that charm can be blinding. Make sure you find a lot more about the person before you even consider a relationship with them.

Examine Your Self-Worth

If you're having problems attracting the kind of partner you would like to be in a relationship with, then you need to explore your feelings of self-worth. According to the Universal Law of Attraction, you can only attract that which you feel worthy of receiving. High self-esteem is critical to your happiness and success because you are a living expression of your belief system.

Your beliefs generate the thoughts and emotions that create all your experiences. Much of your present situation is the result of beliefs programmed by past events. If you want to change your life, you must first change the beliefs about yourself.

What is your reaction when you see a happy couple? Do you think, "I am so happy for them; they inspire me and give me hope that I can have that too!" Or, do you find yourself saying something like, "Please gag me. Look at them. Like I need to be reminded that I don't have a relationship. Get a room!" There are obvious differences between these statements. The latter is probably saying to the Universe, "I am not worthy of having a good relationship, and I am jealous." This negative energy will not bring you the perfect partner. In fact, it will probably repel them.

Take a minute to rate your self-worth on a scale of 1-10 (1 being low and 10 being high). Why did you give yourself that number? Why not higher? Why not lower? What do you feel worthy of receiving in life? Do you think only the lucky people ever find a loving partner and live happily ever after?

Look at the kind of people you have attracted in the past. How have they treated you? If they have treated poorly, then you have to ask yourself "why"? Do you think you deserved that treatment? Why did you put up with it? Don't you think you deserve better in the future?

Live in the Present

Many people spend way too much time either living in the past or worrying about the future. Some may have been the stereotypical high school jock or cheerleader and might think that they left their glory days behind a long time ago. Others have a type-A personality who are always worried about their next investment, career move, or moving up in the world in another way. Others don't like their past and are not hopeful about their future. No matter which category someone is in, the same thing is true: *they are not living in the **now**.*

You exist "now"...***now*** is all there is. "Now" is outside of time. There is no past in which you were incomplete and there never will be a future in which you will become complete. Until you accept that you can only exist in the ever present ***now,*** you will believe that fulfillment awaits you in an illusionary future if you take the proper actions. This belief destroys the experience of ***now***, and you continually live in an illusion.

This very moment is it. Nothing is hidden. All of your hoping and dreaming and planning about how it will be in the future...well, this is how it all turned out. This is all there is. You do not exist in time. You exist in ***self***.

Too many people either pine away for a past relationship or constantly wonder when the next one will come. Meanwhile, they are not enjoying the present. There is always something about every moment that can be loved. Try thinking, "What about this moment can ***never*** be repeated?" When you change your mindset, you change your experience.

Don't forget to ***be in the moment.*** Be fulfilled. Be perfect. Be at peace. Be in balance. You have the power to do this.

Insecurity is a State of Mind

Do you feel insecure if you don't have a romantic partner? If so, why do you think you feel this way? What do you fear? Do you think you can't cope with the situation? Do you think you will never find anyone else to love you?

Insecurity is based in fear. You fear that you will never have "enough." This could be enough love, enough sex, enough control, enough happiness, or enough reassurance that you will find "the one" and live happily ever after.

Instead of fighting insecurity, learn to live with it in harmony. Let's face it: life is insecure. Love is insecure. Throughout our lifetimes, we are all constantly moving from the known to the unknown. You can resist insecurity, but you cannot conquer it. As they say, the only thing constant is change, and change generates insecurity for many people.

How would you feel if you could attain total security in all areas of life? Think about it. Would you be satisfied? Or, would it take away all adventure, suspense and aliveness in your life? People often complain about their problems, but if you took them away, you might as well take away their identity. In other words, problems lead to insecurity, and without that feeling … who are you?

Let's try to imagine what it might be like to attain total security. Your life would probably be boring and mundane. There would be no challenge or aliveness. This lack of challenge or aliveness would probably cause you to dislike the feeling of security. Thus, your insecure feelings are not even logical because you probably wouldn't even like your life if you could be secure.

Instead of fighting insecurity, appreciate it. Think how great it is that you have some unknowns in life. If God Himself came down right now and told you how everything would turn out, that would take away one of the greatest mysteries of life.

Fight Jealousy

For singles who would rather be coupled, it is difficult to not be jealous of people who are in happy, committed relationships. But jealousy is nothing but a fear-based emotion that does not serve you well.

When you are jealous of other people, you are excessively concerned that your life is not—and may never be—the way you want it to be. You want a relationship, but currently you do not have one. That is "what is." When you are jealous, you feel incomplete and believe that only by having a relationship can you be complete. But stop. Step back. Look at it more carefully. This is not a logical point of view. Having a relationship cannot make you complete. You have to feel like a secure and complete person before you can even attract that which you want out of a relationship.

Excessively jealous people often feel like they are not as happy as others. This feeling of jealousy or desperation will actually emanate from you and may drive people away. No one wants to date someone who is ***desperate*** to have a relationship. Instead, they want to date someone who is happy being alone, but ***chooses*** to be with ***them.***

You need to accept that you cannot change the situation. Yes, you can take actions to find another partner (which you should if you want to), but ultimately, you cannot control whether or not you find a good match. It is better to just sit back and enjoy the ride and appreciate the mystery of the outcome. It is difficult to do, but it all starts with you and a change in your mindset. You simply need to see the glass half full, instead of half empty. Once you do that, you will realize that once you change your perspective, you can change your life.

Reserve Judgment

People are quick to judge. They judge everything and anything. If someone has an interaction with a new person with whom they find something distasteful, they will most likely label that person in a negative way. While this isn't a problem in and of itself, if you don't give that person a second chance to prove you wrong, then you might be selling yourself short. You might not get to know someone who is actually a great person.

The quick judgments made sense in the cave man days; people needed to make quick judgments about their surroundings so they wouldn't get eaten by wild animals or attacked by other people. This survival mechanism of our brain does not necessarily serve us well in this day and age.

Here's an example. Let's say you just started a new job. One day, you overhear one of your co-workers teasing another co-worker. You are appalled and decide this guy must be a jerk. You keep your distance. You never get to know him because of that one incident.

What is wrong with the above scenario? Many people would say nothing. But, maybe, that guy is a wonderful, caring person who just likes to innocently tease people. Is it really fair that you labeled this whole person's character based on one interaction? No. To judge others based on such a small observation is not fair, nor is it wise.

Oftentimes people go through this same judgment process when they are dating. They are quick to judge. Maybe it was something they said. Or their less than polite table manners. Or the clothes they wore. Or a whole list of other things. If you quickly dismiss the person from a future date because of one or two things, you might be making a mistake. Instead, reserve judgment and give the person another chance.

Independent or Dependent?

What kind of person are you and what kind of relationship do you want? Some people are very independent. They like their space and don't need constant communication with their partners. On the other hand, some people don't feel loved or connected if they don't see and talk to their partner all the time.

Ask yourself a few questions: How often do you like to talk to your significant other on the phone each day? What about email? Are you more of a phone talker or a writer (email)? Do have a problem going more than an hour without communication or do you find it annoying if someone is in constant contact? How often do you like to see them? Once a week? Once a month? Once a day?

Everyone has different comfort levels. Let's assume you are the kind of person who likes to talk on the phone and see your partner as much as possible. Then, you meet someone who seems to be perfect for you. You email and call them a lot. They talk to you, but they don't take the initiative to call you. They do send you emails quite a bit, but that's just not enough for you. You feel neglected.

This may not be the case. Perhaps that person just has different needs. They may like their space more. Research has found that there are many different kinds of couples. Some like to spend almost all of their time together. Another group likes time together, but still needs their space and their own friends/activities. The final group consists of "separates" who are happy with seeing each other on a minimal basis. The key is finding someone who is like you. If you are someone who likes constant communication and companionship, then you will probably not be happy with someone who is a "separate."

Let it Fizzle

Dating is confusing. It seems like many people can't find someone they like. Or, if they find someone they like, then that person does not like them. When they do finally find mutual attraction and interest, they think everything should be on automatic pilot and roll smoothly. But this doesn't always happen.

There may be times when you find someone you like enough to have a second date with. And third. And fourth. And maybe even have sex with. But maybe there is not enough "sizzle" in your relationship to sustain it. In other words, there may not be enough chemistry—be it at the personality, mental, spiritual, or physical level. Maybe the person is perfect for you "on paper." They are good looking, have a great personality, have a great job, and are seemingly really "into you." You may talk on the phone or text each other all the time. Everything *seems* as if it should be just right. But it isn't.

What should you do in this situation? Keep dating the person? Stress out about why you are not feeling emotionally connected to them? Or just go with the flow?

The correct answer is *go with the flow.* Chances are, this kind of relationship cannot and will not last. It is likely that one of you will pull back—consciously or unconsciously—and it will end eventually. There will probably be excuses (yours or your partners') about being *so busy* or *not ready.* Don't forget to read between the lines. If you just "aren't feeling it," then you probably never will!

Don't be afraid to simply *let it fizzle.* Have faith in the Universe. Have faith in yourself. If you have to force yourself to have feelings for someone, then it's just not meant to be. You deserve the best. You deserve to have the person of your dreams. Let those kinds of relationships fizzle, be patient, and let the Universe bring the ***right*** person to you.

Don't Commit Too Soon

Whenever we meet someone we like, our natural tendency is to shut out all other suitors. Many people think that they shouldn't bother going out with anyone else because they have found someone they like.

Take a look at your life situation. How much time do you have to devote to dating? Many people have very busy lives; they have work, and/or maybe they have children to raise. Where can you fit a relationship into it? It is for this reason, that you should be very picky. If you commit to someone too soon, you make yourself unavailable for others who might be more suitable to come along.

Anyone who has been in a failed romantic relationship (which is pretty much everyone) can tell you that what you see is not always what you get. The person you meet on the first few dates is most likely not the person who will emerge months or years down the road. Or, even if that person doesn't change, there still may be something that will keep you from having a happy, successful long term relationship.

Remember to be cautious. While it sure is fun to jump in the deep end right away, it's not always the best thing to do. If you do this every time after you have a few successful dates, you might also end up jumping into bed with them as well. While that may not be a problem for some people, others may get hurt as a result. Be yourself, but be cautious about the other person.

The best course of action in any situation is to follow your intuition, and your intuition may not always kick in right away. It may take a little getting to know a person before you can really get a feel for whether or not you want to (or should) commit yourself to them.

Don't Encourage "Stalkers"

Some people are too nice, especially women. Females are socialized in our culture to be very polite and friendly to other people. While this is alright in most situations, in others it can get you into trouble.

There are some strange people out there. You've probably even met a few of them, so you know what we're talking about. This is a common scenario: you may go out with someone once or twice until you find out they are really not a match for you. Then, you try to politely say, "I'm not ready" or "You're great person, but I think I'd like to be friends." Some people don't understand that language. They can't read between the lines like the rest of us. If they hear, "I'd like to be just friends," they might respond with: "I like to think of relational boundaries as mutual decisions of desired interaction across several dimensions (spiritual, sexual, emotional, interpersonal, intellectual, etc) — typically with the person with the "coldest feet" setting the limits in each category. We will have to discover the right mix for the two of us, but I think that is half the fun of a new relationship. I would suspect that we will each take turns being the "cold foot" in different areas. It will be interesting to see where our relational energy takes us. I already see a great deal of intellectual connection and a bud of emotional honesty. I have no clue where the others will fall out."

Now, does that response sound like someone who understood, "I just want to be friends?" No. This person didn't know that, "I just want to be friends" really meant, "I'm just not that into you." This person saw it as an opportunity to try even harder. If that's not what you want a person to do, then you need to be blunt.

Take a Break

Everyone handles a break-up differently. Some take some time to be by themselves to heal and re-group their life. Others decide to dive right back into the dating pool. This could be for a variety of reasons. Perhaps, they are so relieved to have the bad relationship over with that they can't wait to meet new people. Or, they are living in denial and avoidance; they figure that if they keep themselves distracted with dating, then they won't feel the pain that comes along with the end of a relationship.

Whatever the reason, sometimes dating becomes frustrating, and it can even become a "chore." We've heard people refer to the dating game as a "job," as if it was merely just one "interview" after another. Many people's tendency is to merely keep plugging away at dating until they finally find someone with whom they can begin anew.

If you have come to the point where dating is no longer fun, and you have to force yourself to get excited about the next date, then *stop doing it. It's okay to be alone.* In fact, being alone can be quite refreshing. You don't have to deal with all the people out there who make dating difficult.

Take time off. Take a break. Re-group your life. Find yourself. For some people, dating is fun and an adventure. For others, it is just disappointing because they never seem to find "The One."

If you take a break, you will get more in touch with yourself. Once you learn more about yourself and what you want, you will be more likely to attract the right person. Don't forget to *enjoy* the break. Live in the moment!

RADICAL TIPS

FOR LETTING GO & MOVING ON

The tips in this sub-section of "Letting Go & Moving On" are **RADICAL**

You will need an open mind and a curious spirit (or at least a sense of humor) to read these tips!

Investigate Your Future Lives

Time is an illusion: it doesn't exist. That statement is probably one of the most difficult for all humans to grasp. However, it has been scientifically proven. Einstein discovered the phenomenon of relativity. So even though it seems like we are bound by linear time, we are not.

With that in mind, your soul is actually living all of its lives ***right now***. In other words, the way we traditionally think of reincarnation is not accurate. Reincarnation implies a linear progression from lifetime to lifetime. But since time is an illusion, this life you are now living is ***both*** your ***past and future lives.***

Here is a good analogy. Imagine a multi-leveled chess board. Each level has its own game being played, and each of these games is analogous to one "lifetime." However, the main difference between a regular chess game and this multi-faceted one is that each game is going on simultaneously, and a move on one level affects all other games.

What this means is that your actions, today, right now, are influencing your past lives ***and*** your future lives. Just as the "negative karma" that was incurred is affecting you now, the karma you are creating today is also affecting your future lives.

Therefore, investigating your future lives can be of use to your relationship. You can find out what kind of karmic effects you and your partner are creating right now, and how it is affecting your future incarnations. If the future "yous" are experiencing hardship with your partner, then the chances are that you are not doing a very good job at working things out. You will need to change your actions now or else you are destined to return with your mate until you both can learn to express unconditional love.

You can investigate your future lives the same way as you do your past. By seeing hypnotherapist or using a CD, you can use hypnosis to uncover answers. Receiving such knowledge will help you enhance your relationship with your mate for the better so you only have to come back with him/her if you ***want to***, not because you ***have to***.

Make Contact with Your Future Self

Time is an illusion: it does not exist. This can be used to your advantage when it comes to your relationship. Similar to investigating your future ***lives***, you can also make contact with your future ***self.***

At one time or another, we have all said to ourselves, "If only I knew that back then, I could have changed things." This concept is the basis for this repair. It allows you a "do over." Your future self probably has a lot of great advice to give you about your relationship.

Let's say you are Kate Olsen reading this book right here in the current year. You are 43 years old, have two children, and have been married to your husband for sixteen years. While you were happily married in the beginning, in the last five years, your husband has become distant and unloving.

So you are sitting here in this year wondering what actions you should take to rectify the situation. Should you go to counseling? Should you get a divorce? Should you simply sit back and do nothing?

You can answer some of these questions by contacting yourself in the future. This does not mean contacting yourself in a future incarnation. Instead, you will be contacting Kate Olsen in another year, such as 2020. This can be done either by automatic writing or through meditation.

In automatic writing, you would either do self hypnosis or use a CD to induce a light trance. You would want to make clear which future self you would like to talk to (or you could simply let your higher self choose). Then you should sit back, relax, and let the pen start moving on its own.

Awareness of "Soul Switching"

Most religions and, therefore, most people, believe that one soul inhabits a body for the duration of a lifetime. However, some metaphysically-oriented people believe "Soul Switching" occurs. This can take on many forms and can wreak havoc on relationships.

Many years ago, best-selling author Ruth Montgomery wrote about "Walk-Ins." A "walk-in" is a soul who trades places with the soul that originally inhabited the body. This usually occurs when the first soul has come to a point where they do not want to continue living. So, it switches places with another soul that wants to step in and, for humanitarian reasons, live out the body's biological life. The new soul retains all the memories of the original soul, so he/she does not realize a transfer has taken place.

Another form of soul switching is when two or more souls decide before birth to share a body. It's like sharing a text book for a class you are taking: the text book is the body, and the people sharing the book are the "students." The form it takes varies. In some cases, one soul will begin the life, and the other one will end it. Or, perhaps, they will continuously switch off through the lifetime.

One common denominator to all soul switching is a noticeable change in personality. This can be for the better, or it can be for worse. Humans rationalize the switching of souls with logical reasons for the change. We blame personality changes or relationship problems on outside circumstances instead of on the switching of souls.

How would you know if this happened in your relationship? Work with a metaphysical hypnotist or learn automatic writing.

Use Automatic Writing to Find Answers

Automatic writing is a method of making contact with the spirit world. It is a form of channeling. There are many words for this phenomenon, such as the ever-so-popular "medium," but the purpose and outcome are all the same no matter what it is called.

In automatic writing, you either use self hypnosis or an Automatic Writing CD to induce a light trance. You visualize a protective, white, God light so that only very highly evolved and loving entities who mean well will be able to communicate through your hand during the automatic writing session.

Once you are settled with a pen in your hand and notebook on your lap, write your question at the top of the page. Also, write the name or source of information you desire to communicate with. It could be a loved one who is now in spirit, your Higher Self, your Spirit Guide, or Guardian Angel. Or, it could be a specific person in spirit that you feel you could learn from. Be careful who you ask for. Just because someone is in the history books, doesn't mean they were spiritually evolved.

Once you're in an altered state of consciousness, barely open your eyes and prepare for the writing to begin. We advise that you make slow ovals on the paper so you maintain an open energy flow. You may want to begin by writing any thoughts that come into your mind. This often leads to automatic writing.

Automatic writing is a skill. We have to practice our tennis strokes if we want to be a good tennis player, and we have to practice at automatic writing if we want to develop the ability. Some people will have a more natural talent than others, but everyone should be able to reach some level of success. It takes some getting used to; however, if it you practice regularly, you will see results, and the technique can give you some great insights.

While automatic writing can be used to receive all kinds of answers about your life, it is especially useful for relationships. The following are several topics that you can use as a guideline: **1|** Past Lives/Negative Karma shared with your partner (past or present), **2|** Overall lessons to be learned with your partner (or a future one), **3|** Reasons your souls decided to reunite in this life, **4|** Individual specific lessons you are both learning, and **5|** Suggested actions or approaches to improve the relationship.

Investigate Your Destiny

See an Astrologer

How much of our life is pre-destined and how much is free will? Everyone seems to have a different answer to this question, but there seems to be one consistent element: we have both.

Based on the karma we have accrued as a soul, we have to figure out what lessons need to be learned. The goal is to learn how to express unconditional love. There are events that are pre-destined, and there are other areas of our life that are much more open-ended.

Fortunately, we don't have to guess. If you want to know how much of your life is pre-destined, it will help to see a good astrologer. Don't read the general astrological information you find in newspapers or books. Some of it is useful, but to see the plan for your life, you need to see how and where the stars were aligned at the moment of your birth. You will need your birth date, exact birth time, and location.

Astrology won't tell you everything, but it is likely that the astrologer will see the exact point in your life in which you met your partner and may even be able to predict if your relationship will end. Either way, you may be able to figure out what lessons need to be learned with your mate.

If you have learned everything you can from this relationship, it may be time to let it go and move on. Knowing something is destined can often help you to accept it. Or your chart might indicate that you and your partner will be together for life. If so, your soul has set up the union for the learning potentials you will experience.

A good astrologer can often provide you with peace of mind about your future or at least give you a heads up in regard to what's coming.

Protect Yourself from Psychic Attacks

We are all psychic — whether we know it or not. People who are considered to be good at it can easily "pick up" thoughts other than their own.

Thoughts are energy. They can be photographed, and their vibration can be measured. Therefore, they exist in a scientific, logical, and objective sense and have the power to affect others, and vice versa.

Perhaps, your relationship is being negatively affected by outsiders' psychic attacks. In Dick's book *Past Lives, Future Loves*, he recounts fascinating case histories on this topic. He says, "Thought projection affects everyone, but when directed at someone with a psychic sensitivity, or empathic tendencies, the effects can be very strong." In fact, Dick has done many studies on people where their own personal lives were being affected and upset by telepathic projections. Most of these people weren't psychic or particularly empathic themselves.

In the same book, he explains this case study, "Case A: An ex-husband was purposely using mental techniques learned through his involvement with one of the country's foremost awareness-expanding organizations, to psychically attack his former wife. He had not wanted the divorce, and once the marriage was formally dissolved, he told her that he would destroy her. The techniques could be called by many names, but they all amount to "black magic." Within a few months, the woman was unable to eat, to concentrate on her job, and was experiencing physical pains."

Most people don't give consideration to psychic phenomenon. The power of thought and psychic attack is very real. The scary part of it is that you may never be aware of what is happening. There is a possibility that someone is, either knowingly or unknowingly, attacking your relationship.

If you suspect this to be the case, then you need to use spiritual protection. If done daily, you can usually nullify effects of such attacks.

Taking A Lover

As counselors and seminar trainers, we often hear of relationships in which one partner wants little or no sex with their mate/lover. The other partner climbs the walls in need of orgasmic release through intimate interaction. When this is not available, the more highly-sexed partner often resentfully masturbates and/or has an affair. The affair, if exposed, usually generates angry communications, which further weaken or destroy the relationship.

Approximately 50 percent of US marriages will end in divorce. Looking at the divorce rates for 35 countries, the US is at the top, and Italy, a country where taking a lover is accepted as part of life, is number 34.

Sexual morality, as commonly accepted in America, is based upon archaic religious ideas and the 35-year life spans of the Middle Ages. Such thinking and statistics do not relate to modern times. Strict monogamous pairings is not the only relationship option. If one person wants more sex than the other, "opening" the relationship might be an option. If a couple wants to stimulate their sex life, "opening" the relationship might also be an option.

Polyamory is a term to describe all forms of multi-partner relating. "Loving More" magazine says polyamory is for people who wish to live outside traditional monogamy responsibly and with integrity.

Anthropologist and author Helen Fisher claims anthropological studies of 853 human societies showed only 16 percent practicing monogamy as we typically define it. "You would think that more people would be practicing polyamory," she says. Fisher claims polyamorists have found a way to deal with sexual snags. She adds, however, "Americans are wedded to the notion of lifelong pair bonding. We'll see more divorce and adultery rather than an attempt to channel our urges in an honest way. The majority of Americans will not endorse polyamory, ever."

The Law of Resistance

When people find themselves single, some resist it. They frequently find themselves saying, "I hate being single" or "Look at all the happy couples out there, I wish I had that" or "I am so sick of spending yet another Saturday night alone." Notice the theme in all of those statements: resistance. If you talk like that to yourself or in your conversation with others, then you are resisting "what is."

It's a simple law: ***what you resist, you draw to you***. As long as you resist something, you are locked into fighting it and merely perpetuating its influence in your life. Resistance is fear. You must let go of the fear by fully experiencing and appreciating singlehood. You must ***appreciate*** the opportunity to be alone. As strange as that sounds, that simple act will help release the hold it has on your life. You can do this by consciously detaching yourself from what you view to be a negative situation.

Happy people don't oppose things. Nor do they attempt to change the situation by asserting themselves against it. Instead, they go with the flow. This is the principle of controlling life by going along with it.

Which kind of person are you? Are you the "go with the flow" type or the one who constantly resists? If you do resist, consider this question: Is it helping? Does complaining about being single really find you the mate of your dreams? Of course not. Try to reframe your situation. What if someone told you that Mr./Ms. Right will swoop into your life in six months? Would you spend that six months complaining about the fact that they have not yet arrived? Or, would you cherish the last single months you will ever have as long as you live? Remember, if you do find "the one" and live happily ever after, your single days are over. Appreciate them while you can.

Belief Blocks

One of the first steps to manifest change in your life is to search out the deep-seated beliefs that are blocking you from becoming more. Beliefs generate your thoughts and emotions that create your experiences. Your beliefs are the results of two things: **1**| Present-life programming resulting from experiences and influences with parents, siblings, friends, church, society, etc. and **2**| Past-life experiences.

Pinpointing surface core beliefs dictates who and what you are and how this relates to your relationships or lack of relationships, career, success and everything central to your existence.

You can't change what you don't recognize. In our seminars, we teach techniques to become aware of blocking beliefs. Here's a simple technique that will allow everyday experience to supply the awareness:

Your emotions are communicating a message. Every emotion is created by (and symbolizes) a belief. Take a moment to recall a fully experienced emotion. Now explore the belief behind the emotion; this will explain your reaction.

As an example, Alex got angry when his wife took too long getting ready to accompany him to a restaurant. In tracing his emotion back to his belief, he realized that he believed his mate should be concerned with the discomfort he experienced when forced to wait. His wife did not do what he expected her to do, which, in his mind, amounted to a lack of love on her part. Looking a little deeper, it's easy to see that Alex believes a husband has the right to control his wife—a faulty assumption that could undermine his marriage.

Your emotions are a form of energy that generates ever-changing states of feeling, which dovetail into each other. Once you're aware of your core beliefs, catch yourself every time you experience a negative belief coming into your mind. Reverse the programming power by consciously expressing a contrasting positive belief. For most of us, growth takes a bit of effort but well worth it.

Write a Thank You Letter to the Universe

(The Law of Gratitude)

As early as the 1930s, scientists have proven that thoughts and emotions are real. They are energy; they can be photographed and their rate of vibration can be measured. The general conclusions of these studies have been that emotions and thoughts can affect your reality for better or worse. Moreover, the more positive the emotion, the faster it vibrates. Likewise, the more negative an emotion, the slower it vibrates.

The emotions that vibrate the fastest are love and gratitude. They are the most powerful in terms of creating the reality you desire. Think about it: people tend to love others who passionately love them. We tend to give freely to people who truly appreciate our acts or gifts. It is human nature. It is also how the Universe works.

Whatever you give thanks for will only increase. Being grateful for "simple" things in your life is important. Unfortunately, most people (at least in our culture) take the everyday things for granted: shelter, food, warmth, comfort, and companionship. Most of us have never known life without the basic necessities, so we rarely think to be thankful for them. But the more you express appreciation to the Universe, the more you can be assured that you will always have what you need and desire.

This Law of Gratitude can be applied to your relationship, which is one of the "simple" things in life for which most people don't give appreciation. It is more likely that you focus on how your partner is irritating you, instead of the good things he/she does. However, this focus only perpetuates the negatives.

Your partner will improve his or her behavior if you write a thank you letter to the Universe describing all the wonderful things about them. It re-focuses your energy in order to emit more positive vibrations, and it also shows the Universe that you want the good things to continue.

About Carol Morgan & Dick Sutphen

DR. CAROL MORGAN brings the general and academic perspective to this book. She holds a Ph.D. from the University of Nebraska, and is a Professor in the Department of Communication at Wright State University. Relationships are one of her main areas of expertise. She has presented her research all across the country, and has also been a trainer and consultant for businesses such as AdvoCare, Delphi International, and Girl Scouts of America. Dr. Carol has personally taught thousands of people her life-changing relationship techniques through seminars, e-courses, radio, and television. She is also the author of *We're not that Different: Two Sisters' Religious and Spiritual Journeys* and co-hosts Dick's radio show every month (*Dick Sutphen's Metaphysical World*). Dr. Carol is also a regular motivational expert on the TV show *Living Dayton*. Find her at: www.DrCarolMorgan.com

DICK SUTPHEN brings the radical perspective to this book because of his background in past-life regression, and all things psychic and spiritual. He is the author of the million-copy bestseller, *You Were Born Again to Be Together* (Simon & Schuster). He has also authored 21 New Age books, seven for Simon & Schuster who calls him 'America's Foremost Psychic Researcher.' As a specialist in Past-Life Regression and Spirit Contact Therapy, Dick has conducted psychic and spiritual seminars all across the world. Over a quarter of a million people have attended a Sutphen Seminar. His radio show *Dick Sutphen's Metaphysical World,* (co-hosted once a month with Carol) and is heard by nearly a half a million people each week. Find him at: www.RichardSutphen.com

www.ingramcontent.com/pod-product-compliance
Lightning Source LLC
LaVergne TN
LVHW091053080826
845145LV00002B/728
9780615901466